GETTING A JOB IN

HEDGE FUNDS

GETTING A JOB IN
HEDGE FUNDS

AN INSIDE LOOK AT
HOW FUNDS HIRE

ADAM ZOIA with AARON FINKEL

John Wiley & Sons, Inc.

Published by John Wiley & Sons, Inc., Hoboken, New Jersey.
Published simultaneously in Canada.

For general information on our other products and services or for technical support, please contact our Customer Care Department within the United States at (800) 762–2974, outside the United States at (317) 572–3993 or fax (317) 572–4002.

Wiley also publishes its books in a variety of electronic formats. Some content that appears in print may not be available in electronic formats. For more information about Wiley products, visit our Web site at www.wiley.com.

ISBN 978-0-470-22648-3

Printed in the United States of America

10 9 8 7 6 5 4 3 2 1

CONTENTS

PREFACE

Hedge funds have become some of the most sought-after places to work within the financial markets. Yet, as popular as they are, in many ways hedge funds are still a mystery—both in how they bring on new people and in how they invest their capital. This book focuses on demystifying the first part of the equation—how hedge funds hire. As we do that, we also outline the skills funds look for in candidates. We, of course, *want* you to be excited and will encourage you to pursue your dream job, yet we would be remiss if we didn't caution that getting a job with a hedge fund is extremely difficult. There are simply many more people who want to work at hedge funds than there are openings. In that scenario, the hiring firms can afford to be very selective and bring on only those people who they believe have precisely what it takes to succeed.

Although hedge funds differ significantly depending on their investment style, the goal of all of them is to produce superior risk-adjusted returns for their investors. To work at one, you should ideally be *passionate* about investing. At some funds, you may be able to get away with just being *interested* in investing, but it will not set you apart as much from other candidates. You need to be able to thrive in a pressure-packed environment and work as part of a close-knit group of highly skilled professionals in which the performance of each investment can be measured on a daily basis. If that is the world that you want to be a part of, then this book is for you.

Our aim is to help you best position yourself to improve your chances of getting a position at a hedge fund. To do that, we thought this book should contain more than just our views. As recruiters, we have access to two groups that can help you— the people who have successfully landed positions and the hedge funds that are doing the hiring—and we felt it would be vital to incorporate their views into this guide. The stories of past job candidates whose paths you are looking to follow are presented in the form of case studies. Reading these case studies will give you firsthand accounts of what backgrounds are attractive to hedge funds, what worked and didn't work for these individuals, and what the interview process was like. Although these case studies are anonymous, we feel they still offer unique insight into the job search process. Some of these individuals also agreed to let us publish their resumes. We are grateful to all who shared their stories with us. In addition to the case studies, throughout the text you will also find insight from various senior-level people working in the industry.

Some of these are incorporated into the text and others are presented as sidebars that we call Insider Tips.

As you read this book you will quickly learn that hedge funds take a different approach to hiring than do most other parts of the financial services industry. Don't get us wrong; hedge funds are just as demanding (if not more so) as investment banks, private equity funds, and traditional money managers. The difference lies in the often haphazard way they hire. Although we have seen a growing number of the larger hedge funds moving to a more "on-cycle" system of hiring—meaning they interview in the summer and fall for positions that start the following summer—there are some that have unpredictable needs when looking for entry-level support and thus may hire for immediate starts rather than the traditional summer start dates favored by investment banks (when they hire out of undergraduate and business schools) and private equity firms (when they hire out of investment banking and consulting programs). Note: To learn more on private equity hiring, see *The Glocap Guide to Getting a Job in Private Equity*. If you interview at a hedge fund, you should be aware when your start date would be and how that would affect your current job or training program. Depending on how you look at it, this type of hiring can make your search either easier or harder.

Although there is a chapter on getting into hedge funds later in your career (Chapter V), this book is not designed for the very seasoned professional. Rather, it focuses primarily on entry-level roles for investment professionals, traders, and select noninvestment positions. Chapters II through IV outline the more common entry points for research analysts and traders—directly out of undergraduate school, a few years out of school (pre-MBA), and out of business school. Because hiring is different for some of the other roles at hedge funds and at a fund of hedge funds, we present separate chapters for fund marketers (Chapter VI), risk managers (Chapter VII), operations professionals (Chapter VIII), accountants (Chapter IX), and people looking to get into fund of funds (Chapter X). Finally, there are chapters that outline how to put together a solid resume, what to expect in the interview process, what the latest compensation levels are, and how to get the most out of recruiters.

What this book does not do is take a textbook look at the hedge fund industry. Chapter I, Getting Started, presents a brief look at hedge fund basics and reviews some of the major hedge fund strategies, but that's about as far as we go. We purposely do not take a detailed look at the history of hedge funds, their legal structure, or the regulatory environment in which they operate. If you want to learn more about how Alfred Winslow Jones formed the first hedge fund in 1949 or feel the urge to know how hedge funds invest, we list sources to get that information in Appendix A. Instead, this book focuses on what we do best: counsel qualified job candidates on how to break into the industry.

Throughout this book we mention hedge fund styles wherever possible. We do that because the specific strategy employed by a fund goes a long way to determining the culture of the fund and the skills that will be sought. Although we point out the most appropriate backgrounds for each investment style and how to prepare for interviews, we do not offer any guaranteed strategies for getting a job in hedge funds. There may be things out of your control that you should be aware of; for example, if a major hedge fund implodes it can affect the entire market. We want you to understand the elements that *are* within your control so you can put your best foot forward, because that is what you are going to *have* to do. We can give you all the advice in the world, but at the end of the day getting a job will be up to you, your skills, your knowledge, your professional and academic background, and how you present yourself. If you have the right mix of qualifications and can communicate that effectively, you will be in good shape. Good luck!

ABOUT THE AUTHORS

ADAM ZOIA

Adam is the founder and Managing Partner of Glocap Search LLC and currently runs the firm's hedge fund practice. He has been actively recruiting hedge fund and private equity professionals for almost a decade and has worked on searches for many well-established funds in the United States and Europe. Adam is a frequent speaker at conferences and business schools and has been sought out and appeared on numerous occasions on mainstream media, including CNN and CNBC, as an expert on hiring trends and executive compensation. In addition to this book, Adam spearheads Glocap's annual Hedge Fund Compensation Report.

Adam started his career as an academic, having taught at Harvard College for three years as a Teaching Fellow in Economics, and also worked briefly in management consulting at McKinsey and in investment banking at DLJ. He has a BS in economics from the Wharton School with a concentration in finance (summa cum laude; Joseph Wharton Scholar); a BA in history from the University of Pennsylvania (summa cum laude; Benjamin Franklin Scholar); an Honours BA in politics, philosophy, and economics from Oxford University's Balliol College (graduated with a first on all papers); and a JD from Harvard Law School (magna cum laude).

AARON FINKEL

Aaron is Vice President and Head of Publications at Glocap. In addition to coauthoring this book, Aaron coauthored *The Glocap Guide to Getting a Job in Private Equity*. He also coordinates the research, analysis, and production of Glocap's annual Private Equity and Hedge Fund Compensation Reports and handles all media relations. Aaron has 17 years of experience in financial journalism, 11 years of which were spent at Institutional Investor's newsletters where he worked as a reporter, editor, and publisher. Aaron has covered various topics throughout his career including emerging markets, corporate finance, and asset management. Prior to his time at II, Aaron lived and worked in Venezuela for five years. Aaron graduated from Brandeis University.

GETTING A JOB IN
HEDGE FUNDS

Chapter 1

GETTING STARTED

Consider this your pregame pep talk. Before you take the field and set out on your search for a hedge fund position, there are several fundamental things you must know. You should at least be familiar with what hedge funds are, how they make money, and the role they play in the financial markets. In addition, you will need a solid understanding of the different investing styles. Once you know these things, you will be better equipped to begin your search.

The hedge fund market has grown exponentially over the past several years. Although estimates vary, most agree that there are close to 10,000 funds in operation worldwide. According to Hedge Fund Intelligence, global hedge fund assets hit $2.48 trillion at the end of the first half of 2007. Other sources indicate that as recently as 2001, there were approximately $600 billion in total hedge fund assets, whereas 10 years earlier, in 1991, the number stood at $221 billion.

Even more notable than the growth in sheer numbers of funds and assets under management (AUM) is how the industry has evolved into a significant force in the global economy. To say that hedge funds have developed from a cottage industry into one that plays a major role in the financial markets would be a tremendous understatement. Although $2.48 trillion is a staggering number, that figure dramatically understates hedge funds' influence. When the amount of leverage used by hedge funds and the frequency of their trading are factored in, their net impact is even greater. By managing such large amounts of capital, hedge funds have become major players on many of the world's public markets.

BIGGER AND BIGGER

A semiannual survey of U.S. hedge funds by *Absolute Return* magazine (see Table 1.1 and Table 1.2) found that the four largest hedge fund firms each had more than $30 billion in AUM. In addition to those firms, there were 76 hedge fund firms managing $5 billion or more and 372 with more than $1 billion in AUM. Of those $1 billion+ funds, 246 are based in the United States. And the big funds keep getting bigger. The top five firms—JPMorgan Asset Management (which includes JPMorgan Asset Management and Highbridge Capital Management), Goldman Sachs Asset Management, D. E. Shaw Group, Bridgewater Associates, and Och-Ziff Capital Management—all increased AUM significantly during the 12 months ending July, 2007.

In terms of hedge fund styles, there are more different types of hedge funds operating today than ever before. Some may be considered extremely risky and not for the faint of heart. Others can be more risk averse and just as dependable as a major mutual fund (in select cases some funds have begun acting like mutual funds by charging only management fees). Despite some notable collapses—Amaranth Advisors in 2006 being one of the most noteworthy—most foresee continued growth for the industry.

Table 1.1 Top Ten Single-Manager Hedge Fund Firms (as of July 2007)

FIRM	LOCATION	AUM (BLNS)
JPMorgan Asset Management[a]	New York	$56.20
Goldman Sachs Asset Management	New York	$39.98
D. E. Shaw Group	New York	$34.00
Bridgewater Associates	Westport, CT	$32.10
Och-Ziff Capital Management	New York	$29.20
Renaissance Technologies Corp.	East Setauket, NY	$29.20
Farallon Capital Management	San Francisco	$26.06
Barclays Global Investors	San Francisco	$23.00
Man Investments Limited	London	$21.13
Tudor Investment Corporation	Greenwich, CT	$20.96

Source: *Absolute Return* magazine, used with permission by HedgeFund Intelligence. Copyright 2007.

[a]Including JPMorgan Asset Management ($19.50 bln) and Highbridge Capital ($36.70 bln).

Table 1.2   Billion-Dollar Hedge Funds by Location (July 2007)

City	Number of Billion-Dollar Firms	AUM (Blns) (July 2007)
New York, U.S.	139	$881.00
London	79	$316.00
Connecticut, U.S.	32	$200.00
California, U.S.	24	$109.00
Massachusetts, U.S.	14	$83.00
Texas, U.S.	11	$45.00
Australia	8	$28.00
New Jersey, U.S.	8	$20.00
Paris	7	$24.00
Hong Kong	7	$12.00
Singapore	6	$7.00
Illinois, U.S.	5	$28.00
Japan	4	$7.00
Bermuda	3	$9.00
Russia	3	$5.00
Sweden	3	$8.00
Minnesota, U.S.	3	$17.00
Wisconsin, U.S.	3	$18.00
Norway	2	$4.00
Florida, U.S.	2	$7.00
Georgia, U.S.	2	$13.00
Virginia, U.S.	2	$4.00
Others	14	$48.00
Total*	381	$1892.00

Source: *Absolute Return* magazine, used with permission by HedgeFund Intelligence. Copyright 2007.

*Includes nine firms with more than one headquarters.

WHAT IS A HEDGE FUND?

As someone interested in this industry, you probably know that a hedge fund is a privately managed investment vehicle that has the ability to invest in a wide variety of securities. Unlike mutual funds, hedge funds can use aggressive and advanced strategies to make investments (for example, selling short and using leverage). Most hedge funds have high minimum investment amounts, limiting them to wealthy individuals and institutional investors.

Investors in hedge funds are limited partners (LPs), and because their capital may be locked in for a predetermined time period their investments are relatively illiquid compared to other types of investments. In a hedge fund, the general partner (GP) is typically the person or entity that created the fund and oversees its trading activities and operations. In addition to investment professionals—traders and research analysts—hedge funds (depending on their size) can have large teams of non-investment professionals made up of accountants, operations specialists, legal and compliance professionals, and support staff.

Technically speaking, the primary aim of most hedge funds is to reduce volatility and risk while preserving capital and delivering positive returns in all market conditions. To put it more succinctly, the goal of all hedge funds is to make money—both for themselves and for their investors.

Hedge funds make money for themselves in two ways. First, they charge investors an annual management fee. This fee is typically between 1% and 2% of assets under management. Second, hedge fund managers also receive a percentage of the fund's annual profits. This performance or incentive fee can fluctuate from 10% to as high as 50% in a few cases, but usually ranges between 15% and 30%, with the norm being 20%. The remaining profits go to the LPs. Here's how it works: Take a $1 billion fund with a 2% management fee and a 20% performance fee (often called "2 and 20"). Right off the bat, the fund takes in $20 million from the management fee each year, which is typically used to pay salaries and overhead. If the fund is up 10% in a given year (a $100 million profit) it will earn an additional $20 million in performance fees (20% of the profits) that can be used to pay bonuses to the fund's employees.

In Figure 1.1, we have created an organizational chart for a typical hedge fund. Of course, hedge funds all operate quite differently, and you should refer to the chart as a general guide only. You will find that the organization of a specific hedge fund

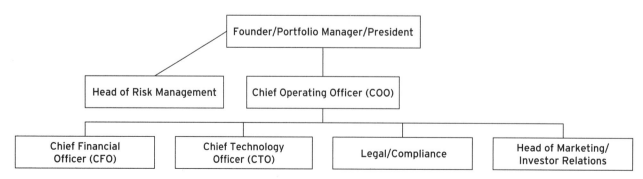

Figure 1.1 Hierarchy of Typical Hedge Fund

depends on, among other things: the size of the fund, if the fund is organized by industry, and whether it is a single profit and loss (P&L) structure or a multi-strategy fund. You will find organizational charts for single P&L and multi-strategy funds in later chapters.

HURDLES AND HIGH-WATER MARKS

Not all funds make money as neatly as in the example just given. It's very possible that a fund can produce stellar returns one year, but be in negative territory the next. To protect LPs, whose money is locked up, some funds have safeguards in place to make sure their own executives are not getting wealthy at the expense of the LPs. In some cases, if a fund is flat or loses money the hedge fund executives will receive little or no monetary rewards, and that's because of the presence of hurdle rates and high-water marks.

Although hurdles are not used too often, the idea is to only reward the hedge fund managers for a return that is greater than an investor could have gotten in a more secure type of investment. Funds that have hurdle rates do not collect a performance (or incentive) fee unless the performance eclipses a predetermined benchmark—the hurdle.

Hedge funds with high-water marks do not receive incentive fees unless the value of the fund tops the highest net asset value previously achieved. For example, if a fund had a net asset value (NAV) of $1 billion at launch and finishes the first year at $1.2 billion, it would collect a performance fee on the $200 million profit, or 20% return. If in the second year the fund loses ground and falls to $1.1 billion, it would not collect a performance fee. If the fund rebounds and rises to $1.4 billion in the third year, LPs would pay a performance fee, but only on the difference between $1.2 billion and $1.4 billion—in this case $200 million. In essence, high-water marks limit hedge fund managers from entering overly volatile trades that allow them to collect a high performance fee one year only to lose LPs' money the next.

HEDGE FUND STYLES

To follow are descriptions of some of the more popular investment strategies (with many of the definitions provided by Lipper HedgeWorld). This list is not meant to be exhaustive. Trading styles (see Table 1.3) come and go as the markets in which they invest evolve (or dissolve). The strategy of the fund will dictate not only the culture of the fund, but the skills sought when hiring. While some strategies have changed over the years (for example, emerging markets funds used to be purely long only but are now more complex), others have stayed the same, and new ones are just developing as we write this guide. There are also many styles that overlap.

Table 1.3 Instruments and Styles

COMMONLY USED INSTRUMENTS	HEDGE FUND STYLES	
Public Equities	Long/Short	Quantitative
Fixed Income	Long Bias	Event-Driven/Special Situations
Currencies	Short Only	Value
Commodities	Arbitrage	Trading Oriented
Derivatives/Futures	Market Neutral	Global Macro
Private Equity	industry Focus	Multi-strategy
Convertible Bonds	Distressed	Geographic Focus

Arbitrage Strategies

There are various types of arbitrage strategies, and all seek to exploit imbalances between different financial markets such as currencies, commodities, and debt. Some of the more popular hedge fund arbitrage strategies are convertible fixed income, risk, and statistical arbitrage.

Convertible Arbitrage

This strategy is identified by hedge investing in the convertible securities of a company. To do this, a hedge fund manager would buy the convertible bonds of a company while at the same time selling (or shorting) the company's common stock. Positions are designed to generate profits from the fixed income security as well as the short sale of stock, while protecting principal from market moves.

Fixed Income Arbitrage

A fund that follows this strategy aims to profit from price anomalies between related interest rate securities. Most managers trade globally with a goal of generating steady returns with low volatility. This category includes interest rate swap arbitrage, U.S. and non-U.S. government bond arbitrage, forward yield curve arbitrage, and mortgage-backed securities (MBS) arbitrage. The mortgage-backed market is primarily U.S.-based, over-the-counter (OTC), and particularly complex. Note: Fixed income arbitrage is a generic description of a variety of strategies involving investments in fixed income instruments, and weighted in an attempt to eliminate or reduce exposure to changes in the yield curve.

Risk Arbitrage

Sometimes called merger arbitrage, this involves investment in event-driven situations such as leveraged buyouts (LBOs), mergers, and hostile takeovers. Normally, the stock of an acquisition target appreciates while the acquiring company's stock decreases in value. Risk arbitrageurs invest simultaneously in long and short positions in both companies involved in a merger or acquisition. As such, they are typically long the stock of the company being acquired and short the stock of the acquirer. The principal risk is deal risk, should the deal fail to close. Merger arbitrage may hedge against market risk by purchasing Standard & Poor's (S&P) 500 put options or put option spreads.

Statistical Arbitrage

Stat arb funds focus on the statistical mispricing of one or more assets based on the expected value of those assets. This is a very quantitative and systematic trading strategy that uses advanced software programs. Note: These funds typically hire PhDs, mathematicians, and/or programming experts.

Emerging Markets

This strategy involves equity or fixed income investing in emerging markets around the world. As emerging markets have matured so too has investing in them. Whereas until recently most emerging markets funds were long only, some of these same funds may now incorporate the use of short selling, futures, or other derivative products with which to hedge their investments.

Equity Strategies

There are several types of hedge funds whose strategies focus on investing in equities. While some of these may use seemingly more traditional strategies, others are quite complex and require very specific skills.

Long/Short Equity

This strategy involves equity-oriented investing on both the long and the short sides of the market. Funds aim to take positions in companies that they believe are undervalued and are therefore trading below their perceived value. Managers have the ability to shift from value to growth, from small- to medium- to large-capitalization stocks, and from a net long position to a net short position. Managers may use futures and options to hedge. The focus may be regional, such as long/short U.S. or European equity, or sector specific, such as long and short technology or healthcare stocks. Long/short equity funds tend to build and hold portfolios that are substantially more concentrated than those of traditional stock funds. Note: This is the most common hedge fund strategy and dates back to the original funds developed in the 1950s. The ultimate goal is to have longs outperform during bull markets and shorts outperform during bear markets.

Dedicated Short Bias

Short bias managers take short positions in mostly equities and derivatives. The short bias of a manager's portfolio must be constantly greater than zero to be classified in this category. Note: Dedicated short sellers were once a robust category of hedge funds before the long bull market rendered the strategy difficult to implement. A new category, short bias, has emerged. The short bias strategy is to maintain net short as opposed to pure short exposure.

Dedicated Long Bias

There are funds that hold only long-term equity positions, much the way a mutual fund invests. By definition, these funds will not short stocks. Practitioners of this style use fundamental bottom-up analysis of a company, technical analysis of the movement of a stock price, or a combination of both.

Equity Market Neutral

This investment strategy is designed to exploit equity market inefficiencies and usually involves being simultaneously long and short matched equity portfolios of the same size within a country so that the return of the fund is uncorrelated with the market return. Market neutral portfolios are designed to be either beta or currency neutral, or both. Well-designed portfolios typically control for industry, sector, market capitalization, and other exposures. Leverage is often applied to enhance returns. Market neutral equity funds, which invest equally in long and short equity portfolios generally in the same sectors of the market, are not correlated to market movement.

Event-Driven Strategies

These strategies are used in equity-oriented investing designed to capture price movement generated by an anticipated corporate event such as a merger, takeover, bankruptcy, or the issuance of debt or equity. Event-driven strategies seek to reduce risk by being uncorrelated to the markets. There are several subcategories within event-driven strategies. These include distressed securities, opportunistic, special situations/value, and Regulation D. Risk arbitrage and high-yield investing are also considered event-driven. Since they overlap with other styles, we give their definitions in the Arbitrage Strategies and Fixed Income Strategies sections, respectively.

Distressed Securities

Fund managers invest in the bank debt, corporate debt, equity, or trade claims of companies undergoing some type of corporate restructuring, reorganization, or distressed sale.

The securities of companies in need of legal action or restructuring to revive financial stability typically trade at substantial discounts to par value and thereby attract investments when managers perceive a turn-around will materialize. Note: The performance of these funds typically does not depend on the direction of the markets. Rather, they aim to profit from the market's lack of understanding of the true value of the deeply discounted securities and because the majority of institutional investors cannot own securities rated below investment-grade.

Special Situations/Value

Fund managers invest in event-driven situations such as mergers, hostile takeovers, reorganizations, or leveraged buyouts. The securities of the target companies are often out of favor or under-followed by the Wall Street research community, but are believed by these funds to be selling at deep discounts to what they believe is their potential worth. Hedge funds that employ this style may simultaneously purchase stock in companies being acquired and sell stock of the acquiring company, hoping to profit from the spread between the current market price and the ultimate purchase price of the company. These funds may also utilize derivatives to leverage returns and to hedge out interest rate and/or market risk. Because they invest in special situations, the performance of these funds is typically not dependent on the direction of the public stock market. Note: This is primarily an equity-based style.

Fixed Income Strategies

There are many different fixed income funds that invest in various types of debt instruments, including mortgage-backed securities (MBS), collateralized debt obligations (CDOs), collateralized loan obligations (CLOs), convertible bonds, high-yield bonds, municipal bonds, corporate bonds, and different types of global securities. There are diversified funds that may invest in a combination of these securities and also arbitrage funds that seek to profit by exploiting pricing inefficiencies between related fixed income securities while neutralizing exposure to interest rate risk.

Convertible Bonds

Convertible bond funds are primarily long only convertible bonds. By definition, convertible bonds are fixed-income securities with the added attraction of giving holders a stock option to buy shares of the underlying company. As the underlying stock rises, the value of the convertible bond should also rise. Investors are protected on the downside, because even if the stock falls, the bond will simply fall to the level where it is in essence a straight bond.

High-Yield

High-yield managers invest in noninvestment-grade debt of companies that show significant upside potential. Objectives may range from high current income to acquisition of undervalued instruments. Managers focus on assessing the credit risk of the issuer. Some of the available high-yield instruments include extendable/reset securities, increasing-rate notes, pay-in-kind securities, step-up coupon securities, and split-coupon securities.

Mortgage-Backed

Mortgage-backed funds invest in mortgage-backed securities. Many funds focus solely on triple-A rated bonds. These can include government agency and government-sponsored enterprise securities, private-label fixed-rate or adjustable-rate mortgage pass-through securities, fixed-rate or adjustable-rate collateralized mortgage obligations (CMOs), real estate mortgage investment conduits (REMICs), and stripped mortgage-backed securities (SMBS). Funds may look to capitalize on security-specific mispricings. Hedging of prepayment risk and interest rate risk is common. Leverage may be used, as well as futures, short sales, and options.

Global Macro

Global macro managers carry long and short positions in any of the world's major capital or derivatives markets. These positions reflect their views on overall market direction as influenced by major economic trends and/or events. The portfolios of these funds can include stocks, bonds, currencies, and commodities in the form of cash or derivatives instruments. Most funds invest globally in both developed and emerging markets. Note: These funds seek to profit from changes in global economies, which are typically triggered by changes in government policy. These changes can affect interest rates and in turn may impact currency, stock, and bond markets. Global macro funds depend on their own fundamental macroeconomic research and often employ a top-down global approach.

Managed Futures

This strategy invests in listed financial and commodity futures markets and currency markets around the world. The managers are usually referred to as Commodity Trading Advisors (CTAs). Trading disciplines are generally systematic or discretionary. Systematic traders tend to use price- and market-specific information (often technical) to make trading decisions, while discretionary managers use a more judgmental or fundamental approach.

Multi-strategy

Multi-strategy investing uses various strategies simultaneously to realize short- and long-term gains. Rather than making dramatic shifts between styles, multi-strategy funds are more apt to reallocate managers within their selected strategies based on the performance of the managers.

Quantitative Strategies

Quantitative funds, which use systematic trading, are highly model-driven and usually rely on detailed software programs to determine when to buy and sell. While most quantitative funds invest in equities, others target fixed-income securities, commodities, currencies, and market indexes. These funds, some of which have billions of dollars in assets, can move the markets in which they invest when an internal buy or sell order is triggered. While quantitative strategies have sometimes produced stellar returns, there have also been some well-known failures of funds using this strategy. Some examples of funds that use quantitative investing strategies are statistical arbitrage, options arbitrage, fixed-income arbitrage, convertible bond arbitrage, mortgage-backed security arbitrage, derivatives arbitrage, equity market neutral, managed futures, and long/short funds.

Sector-Specific Funds

Some hedge fund managers may use any of the aforementioned strategies, but in doing so would focus investments on a specific sector of the market. Managers of these funds usually have both long and short equity positions. As with the strategies discussed earlier, the popularity of sector-specific funds can rise and fall with the markets—one year energy funds may be hot and outperform, and the next they will be out of vogue and real estate may be the sector of choice. Some sectors currently in fashion are energy; financial services; metals and mining; health care/biotech (including medical devices and pharmaceuticals); telecom/media (including fiber optics, telecom services, cable services, entertainment, programming, and broadcasting); real estate; and technology (which may include hardware and software, semiconductors, and networking companies).

DEVELOPING YOUR SEARCH

The market for hedge fund professionals—at both the pre- and post-MBA levels—is as strong as we have seen it in several years, and much of that is a direct result of the tremendous growth of the industry. In fact, we've seen total employment in the hedge fund industry increase each year over the past 10 years. In addition to the growth in assets under management (which has led to more people being needed to invest the capital), there are other factors that have led to increased hiring: The industry overall has become more competitive—there are fewer obvious ways to make money—so it takes more resources (people) to discover investment opportunities; the operational infrastructure of hedge funds has become more sophisticated, creating new functions such as risk management, compliance, fund marketing, operations, and accounting; and many firms have gone global and have hired more people to staff overseas offices.

As the hedge fund industry has grown and matured, so too have the hiring practices of individual funds. Whereas several years ago a large majority of hiring was accomplished through personal contacts and networking, hedge funds are now doing more proactive recruiting, and this is especially evident at the junior level. Hedge funds now actively use search firms to source pre-MBA hires and conduct their own on-campus recruiting at business schools, much like their private equity brethren have done for the past 10 years.

Although the hiring process is more developed than it was just a few years ago, in many ways it is still evolving. The industry still lacks specific hiring cycles and a systematic interview process. Some funds hire new people each year, whereas others hire more sporadically. This book will help point out the similarities that we have noticed across the hedge fund industry. Despite the increased hiring, there is still no typical trajectory for a hedge fund professional. However, once you are in, there may be nothing pushing you out (unless of course the fund closes or blows up). If you are successful, you can make a career out of one hedge fund, start your own fund, go to business school, make a move to another area of financial services, or leave the industry altogether. It's really up to you.

Once you have a solid understanding of hedge funds and hedge fund styles, you should be ready to proceed with the meaty part of your job search. Headhunters intermediate quite a lot in this business, so getting in touch with a recruiter that specializes in hedge funds early in the process would be beneficial (Chapter XIV goes over in more detail our tips for how to work with a recruiter). One of the first things we do when someone tells us they want to work at a hedge fund is gauge their interest. Thus, before you even reach out to a recruiter or contact a hedge fund on your own, there are several things you should be asking yourself, including:

- Do you have what it takes to work at a hedge fund? (Do you even know what it takes?)
- What are your reasons for wanting to work at a hedge fund?
- What style is appropriate for your skills and background?
- What investment ideas do you have?

If you choose to work with a recruiter, you will likely have a preliminary meeting before being sent on an interview with a hedge fund. In that case you will be expected to be able to answer questions such as:

- Why are you interested in hedge funds?
- Have you ever invested on your own before? If so, could you present an investment idea? (This could be your most successful or least successful investment, your most recent one, or your very first one. The actual investment idea is not as important as your ability to explain succinctly why you invested and what your thought process was.)
- If you have not invested on your own before, could you walk through an investment that you *would* have made if you had had the time and money? (Maybe you didn't have enough money, had student loans to repay, or were restricted from investing by your employer. You should at least be able to walk through an investment that you would have made if you had had the time and money. You should be thinking as a potential investor regardless of your current limitations.)
- What type of hedge fund are you interested in? Why? (You should know the differences between the strategies.)
- If you are in an investment banking program or have investment banking experience, you should be prepared to talk about the deals listed on your resume. That includes every detail, including the drivers of the deal.

In addition to looking inward to determine your interests and skills, we recommend reading as much as possible about the subject. In addition to getting you well versed in the vernacular of the hedge fund industry, reading magazines, newspapers, and web sites will keep you up-to-date with the themes in the market and the events that are affecting it. Being well read will also help you prepare for your initial recruiter interviews and those with hiring firms.

We often find ourselves dispelling one of the common misconceptions about hedge funds: that they are all the same. Unfortunately, when most people think of hedge funds they envision a trading fund that places large bets on stocks, currencies, bonds, and various commodities and use lots of leverage when making investments. They see a fund that has a penchant for risk and can be very volatile. However, all hedge funds are not alike, and only a small number are what we would call trading firms. As pointed out earlier, there are many different types of hedge funds, and each can differ significantly from the others. In fact, nearly one-third of all hedge funds are long/short equity funds and, as such, the research they do is very similar to that of any publicly traded mutual fund. They may purchase bigger stakes and some may even take active roles in the direction of the company, but as long-term investors they are not the trading firms that some imagine.

Who Gets In?

As you read this guide, you will notice that the advice we give doesn't differ much for the various entry points. Hedge funds are aware that analysts coming out of banking and consulting programs will be less experienced than individuals with advanced degrees and that those hired out of business schools will be more experienced. In all cases, however, the type of individual coveted by hedge funds is pretty similar. As recruiters, we can easily spot the person who has the personality, skills, academic and professional background, and other intangible factors that appeal to specific types of hedge funds. And, just as important, the professionals at hedge funds can sense very quickly if a candidate has what it takes.

Insider Tip ▷

Senior Hedge Fund Analyst
"Long/short funds want people with investing experience, credit funds want fixed-income experience, and quant funds want mathematicians/ programmers. We have one super stat arb group, and unless you are a PhD you shouldn't think about working there."

You will also notice that it is hard to give blanket advice for all hedge fund styles, because they are all so different from each other. Some funds will accept candidates out of undergraduate school, while others want only PhDs. Some are open to hiring MBAs, while others never tap business schools for talent. There are funds that insist candidates have an intricate understanding of the public stock markets, and there are others that seek individuals with strong math and programming skills only. Instead of going into detail about the skills sought by each specific strategy, we will point out the most common traits that all hedge funds desire.

No matter the investing style, the candidates who will typically draw a lot of interest are those who are absolutely passionate about the markets and are driven, hardworking, thoughtful, and analytical individuals. These are the people who enjoy investing. Not only do they read the *Wall Street Journal* (and may have been doing so from a young age) and other financial publications, but they have their own portfolio, know how to track it and can talk intelligently about their investments. They can recite what is happening in major financial markets because they are interested in them, not because facts were memorized for an interview. These individuals already know the different hedge fund styles and which is a fit for their skills.

Insider Tip ▷

Senior Fund Executive
"If you are looking for a junior role, you need to communicate that you are smart and understand an investment process and how it relates to a specific fund's clients. By that I mean if you go into a growth shop you will need growth ideas and if you go into a value or emerging market shop you cannot go in with quick trading ideas."

Why Investing Is Important

You will read many times in this guide about the importance of investing, and for most hedge funds that means you will need an intimate knowledge of the public markets. How better to get that than to be an investor? A candidate who has been investing will immediately have an advantage. If you have not been investing (even a paper or mock portfolio), we recommend you start.

<table>
<tr>
<td>Glocap Insight</td>
<td>Those who never bought a stock and never followed the markets should think long and hard about why they want to work at a hedge fund. If it's because you have a friend who works at a hedge fund, that will not get you far. This type of person will draw little interest. Have you ever read a book about hedge funds?</td>
</tr>
</table>

Some investment banking analysts tell us that they can't invest because they have no money. And, even if they had the funds, they insist they have no time and the regulations of their banks prohibit them from investing in the markets. All of that may be true, but it's not an excuse. If you interview at a long/short equity fund you will be at a distinct disadvantage if you have no investing experience, so we strongly suggest that you get some. Of course, there are exceptions. For example, for those who have knowledge of credit derivatives it is not as important to have been investing in the public equity markets, as they will likely be recruited by a credit-oriented fund. Similarly, for quantitative funds investing experience is not as relevant as are mathematics and programming skills.

The Analyst Role

Even though the situation differs from fund to fund, as the market has become more competitive most hedge funds have decided they need more analytical horsepower, not less. So, analysts have increased in popularity at hedge funds in the past few years, and that has created more of a typical pyramid structure. Many funds hire analysts as generalists, but as they attract more capital and become larger they also tend to develop a traditional forward path for advancement.

Anyone hired at a junior level would come in as an analyst and would provide leverage for a more senior member of the firm. In the beginning, most analysts at smaller funds are generalists. That means helping analyze companies and coming up with ideas, but more typically as an analyst you would do research for a senior member of the firm. You might be told something like: "Here's an idea—go take a look at it." That includes analyzing a potential investment, breaking it down, modeling it, visiting the business, and talking to some suppliers. Analysts are basically doing the analytical work that goes into making decisions—research analysis.

Pre-MBA versus Post-MBA

Throughout this guide you will read about pre-MBA and post-MBA jobs. Although these sound like they revolve around business school, they do not and should not be taken literally. We separate jobs into "pre-MBA" and "post-MBA" to distinguish between the experience needed to get the jobs and the type of work that will be done. We define pre-MBAs as those people who have generally been out of undergraduate school for five years or less regardless of whether they plan to go to business school. It may be easier to think of this simply as a more junior role at a hedge fund. Post-MBAs are those candidates with anywhere from five to 15 years of total work experience and could include individuals who never went to graduate school.

Chapter II

OUT OF
UNDERGRADUATE SCHOOL

As someone in college you're probably thinking about the first step of your professional life after graduation. You may have watched hedge funds grow into a $2 trillion industry and want to know if you have a chance to be a part of it.

There are some select funds that are open to hiring undergraduates. We have also seen some global macro funds take people directly out of undergraduate school, as those types of funds do not use a bottom-up approach to picking stocks and can therefore bring on people without financial modeling experience. Quantitative funds have also been known to hire undergraduates, but would focus exclusively on individuals with exceptional mathematics and programming abilities. Some funds that may need execution-only traders could also be willing to bring on and train a raw person. The thinking is that traders don't need the same skills as researchers—for example, how to build a discounted cash flow (DCF) model—and therefore wouldn't necessarily have to go through an investment banking program.

Notwithstanding the types of funds mentioned, when bringing on junior staff most firms focus on individuals with some investment banking and/or investing experience. Remember, most hedge funds are smaller organizations as compared to investment banks and don't have the infrastructure to train graduates themselves. Unfortunately, the general perception among hiring firms (and the one mentioned in many of the case studies in this book) is that someone coming out of college doesn't have the right skill set to make it in hedge funds, and we therefore tend to encourage undergraduates to take the appropriate measures to improve their chances of getting into a hedge fund *later on* once they have acquired more skills. To us that means taking the right undergraduate courses, continuing to hone your investing expertise (or developing it if you haven't invested before), targeting the right summer jobs, and working toward the ultimate goal of getting into a top investment banking—or even consulting—program once you graduate. We do include a case study of one person who got into a hedge fund directly out of undergraduate school (Case Study 22), but he benefited from a family contact and even he admits that what he did is rare.

BE AN INVESTOR

Many of our clients tell us they want to see people who have demonstrated sincere interest in the public markets. Thus, having a history of investing will improve your chances of getting into a hedge fund no matter when you break in. You should have your own individual portfolio and be trading it. The dollar amount is not important—it can be $2,000, $5,000, or $10,000; it's more important that you are actively evaluating stocks, making choices, and trading. If you don't have enough real money to invest, at least set up a mock portfolio, as that will demonstrate a genuine curiosity in investing and will give you a leg up, especially for hedge funds whose strategy involves stock picking. (Note: This is true at all entry points into hedge funds, not just out of undergraduate school.) We also recommend joining your school's investment club (if it doesn't have one, think about starting one). Being part of an investment club will show your enthusiasm for investing (and *starting* one will demonstrate a lot of initiative).

HIT THE BOOKS

If you're reading this as a sophomore or even a junior, you still have time to take additional steps to make yourself attractive to hedge funds (and investment banking/consulting programs), and part of that includes taking the right academic courses. If you're not already doing so, you should be studying economics and accounting, as hedge funds will want you to be able to work your way through a balance sheet. We suggest targeting a degree in business, economics, or anything quantitatively oriented such as mathematics, engineering, or sciences. Hedge funds often believe that if you're quantitatively oriented you can figure out financial modeling and balance sheets. We've seen some global macro funds that were willing to look at undergraduates with degrees in economics, mathematics, engineering, sciences, and computer science.

THE FIRST STEP: AN ANALYST PROGRAM

From our experience, working as an analyst in an investment banking program is the most straightforward first step to breaking into a hedge fund, and thus much of the discussion in this chapter revolves around what it takes to get into such a program. Even though your perception of a hedge fund may be that of a trading firm, as we discussed earlier many are long-term equity holders and, therefore, there is a heavy valuation component to the due diligence they do. Many aspects of hedge fund investing are about looking at stocks and constructing financial models. It won't matter if the fund's strategy is event-driven or long/short; junior staffers will most likely be digging into financials as they analyze potential investments. Since very few (if any) hedge funds are prepared to teach you how to construct financial models, they value the financial modeling skills that you would learn in an analyst training program. In short, hedge funds know what they're getting with someone who has gone through a top banking program—a candidate who is skilled in financial modeling, knows accounting, and is comfortable reading a company's balance sheet and financials.

Insider Tip ▷

Hedge Fund Analyst

"If someone still in undergrad told me they wanted to work at a hedge fund, the first thing I would do is ask why. And the answer has to be convincing. You can't just show a passing interest in what hedge funds do. Funds can easily tell when someone is faking interest. If you're truly interested in investing, then it will be something you think about all the time. You may be walking down the street and see a little market and think to yourself, 'I wonder how much they pay in rent, how much food spoilage they have, what their payroll is, and so on.' Telling me you follow stocks on Yahoo! Finance is not showing as much interest in investing as is saying you enjoy diving into business models and analyzing what makes companies run. The second thing I would do is recommend spending two years in investment banking, all the while looking at and assessing business models. That will be the clearest channel to the best funds."

POSITIONING YOURSELF FOR AN ANALYST PROGRAM

We estimate about 2,000 to 2,500 undergraduates are hired each year into midsize to large investment banking and consulting programs in the United States. All the major investment banks have such analyst training programs, as do most of the regional and middle-market banks and the leading consulting firms. (Note: The largest or most elite investment banks are typically referred to as "bulge-bracket" banks.) Based on our own research, in 2007 alone the leading investment banks, including Bear Stearns, Citigroup, Credit Suisse, Goldman Sachs, JPMorgan Chase, Lehman Brothers, Merrill Lynch, and Morgan Stanley, combined brought about 900 first-year analysts into their U.S. offices. On the consulting side, about 400 first-year analysts were on the payrolls of such firms as Bain & Company, Boston Consulting Group, McKinsey & Company, and the Monitor Group.

Securing a spot in an investment banking or consulting program is not easy, especially if the firms do not recruit on your campus. But, taking the right courses in school and getting the right summer experiences will put you on the right path. The analyst programs value strong summer work experiences, so we strongly suggest making optimal use of your breaks. In particular, we recommend targeting a formal banking internship during the summer after your junior year of college. Getting one of these internships can play a pivotal role in securing a spot in a banking or consulting program after graduation. In fact, we've seen candidates enter their senior year of college with an offer in hand for a position in an analyst training program from the same firm at which they interned during the summer, thus saving them from going through the formal interview process. Wouldn't that take some of the stress off your senior year? And who knows? There could even be a hedge fund that may look at you and say, "Ok you spent three months putting together financial models, so at least you have a clue," and offer you a position once you graduate.

Insider Tip ▷

Hedge Fund Analyst
"I quickly found that the best thing one can do to get into an investment bank after college is to do investment banking in the summer. Spending the summer at an accounting firm can also make you attractive to an investment bank."

Getting a banking internship following your junior year will be easier if you have previous hands-on finance experience. We recommend starting as early as the summer following your sophomore year. In particular, we advocate getting some type of position that will expose you to finance—be it at an investment bank or the finance division of a public company. Another summer option is a job with a long-only asset management firm. Such a position will expose you to the public stock markets and serve as a good introduction to life on the buy side. These summer jobs are not mandatory requirements, but they are helpful and banking/consulting programs look favorably on those who have used their summers wisely.

HEDGE FUND INTERNSHIPS

It's fine to go after a summer position at a hedge fund; however, be aware that these opportunities are few and far between. If this is your goal, we suggest checking with alumni from your school who may have started a hedge fund. Why not offer to work for free? At least it will get you some experience. Even if you do land a position, though, there is no guarantee the fund will invite you back for a full-time role after you graduate. Remember, most funds are small groups; so, while they may welcome the summer help, they may simply have no room for a full-time hire. Nevertheless, spending a summer at a hedge fund will certainly be seen as a plus when you apply to a banking/consulting program after college. It will also show you are passionate about the industry, and that could be useful two years down the road when you get out of your analyst program.

OTHER OPTIONS

If you are a senior and did not use the prior summer to your advantage, you may have to play catch-up by widening your search of investment banks or nonbank alternatives that will accept you. If you don't get into an investment banking or consulting program, all hope is not lost. Accounting firms have transaction and valuation groups that also involve heavy financial modeling and can be a lead-in to hedge funds. We know of some funds that are open to consultants.

CHOOSING THE RIGHT BANKING GROUP

Once you are accepted into an analyst program, the group in which you are placed could determine how attractive you will be to hedge funds. Your goal should be to get into a group that will teach you the skills most translatable to working at a hedge fund. In our opinion, these include the investment banking group, mergers and acquisitions (M&A), and leveraged finance. Working in an industry-specific group could also benefit you if you want to stay in that same industry at a hedge fund. We go into more detail about which groups appeal to the specific hedge fund styles in the next chapter.

WHAT IF I GET AN OFFER?

If you do get into a hedge fund straight out of undergraduate school, you should think hard about whether it is the right choice for you at this point in your career. It sounds good to skip a banking program and go straight to a hedge fund, but it may be hard for you to transition to another fund later on. We're not saying you should turn down an opportunity; just think about its merits. Remember, a hedge fund could go under or close down, or you may just feel it is time to move on—maybe the fit is not what you thought it would be. No matter the reason, if you want to stay in the industry other funds will want to know what you learned and may wonder about the extent of your training if it was all in-house. Think about it. You may have proven you can work at a fund with six or seven people, but you may not have been trained to work in another environment. Most likely you have not been making stand-alone investment decisions and therefore have no track record to pitch to other funds. If you worked at a $50 million shop, another $50 million shop *may* be willing to bring you on, but it's doubtful that a $5 billion fund will.

Chapter III

PRE-MBA

When hiring at the pre-MBA level, most hedge funds focus exclusively on candidates in analyst programs at investment banks and consulting firms. However, we have also seen hedge funds hire slightly more seasoned analysts out of private equity (PE) firms. This chapter outlines the pre-MBA recruitment process and presents case studies of people who made it in at this stage. Note: *Pre-MBA* is a term that we use to denote a more junior role at a hedge fund suitable for someone out of undergraduate school for five years or less, and doesn't necessarily mean that all candidates at this level eventually attend business school.

As the hedge fund market has grown and become more institutionalized, firms have had more of a need for junior talent and have become more aggressive about hiring at the pre-MBA level. We estimate that as recently as three years ago only 20% of the recognizable hedge funds hired at this level. Today, we estimate that closer to 75% of those same funds bring on junior staffers. This is a new and still-evolving phenomenon that we expect will continue to impact the hiring process at this level.

Although most hedge funds have no real hiring cycle, we have noticed that some have begun to make systematic year-on-year hiring plans the way leveraged buyout (LBO) funds do, but those are still a distinct minority. Instead, many do what we call on-demand hiring. In essence, they wake up in the morning and say, "I need more people and I want them now," and that is quite evident at this level. Anyone targeting hedge funds will have to understand and work with that haphazard process.

OUT OF AN ANALYST PROGRAM

From our experience placing candidates into hedge funds, coming out of an investment banking analyst program is the number one point of entry. Hedge funds see these junior professionals as prescreened candidates who have a good work ethic, possess finance skills, and are still junior enough to be managed and molded into the types of investors they want. If you are currently in one of these programs, you should, however, take nothing for granted and would be wrong to expect that hedge funds will roll out the red carpet for you. If you haven't guessed it already, you will soon see that the competition is fierce. Hedge funds know how badly people want to work for them and can therefore be extremely picky. They look for the very best talent and have rigid standards for the candidates they choose to interview. You will be subjected to multiple rounds of interviews in which you will be scrutinized and picked apart by many people before an offer is extended.

> ### Glocap Insight
>
> Most hedge funds are looking for people with good interpersonal skills who went to a top-tier school, worked at a bulge-bracket bank, achieved good grade point averages (GPAs) and solid SAT scores, legitimately invested in the markets, and currently actively follow the markets. They want top-ranked analysts and want people with raw talent. To us, those people would be no-brainer hedge fund placements.

Although there are no specific figures on the number of analysts hired each year out of banking programs, we can safely say that there are many more candidates than there are positions available (as we mentioned earlier, our own research shows that about 2,000 to 2,500 undergraduates are hired each year into midsize to large investment banking and consulting programs in the United States). The question becomes how many of those candidates can meet the stringent requirements of hedge funds.

For all candidates, funds will examine every aspect of your background while paying particular attention to undergraduate GPAs, SAT scores, and what school you went to, and will want to see excellence in job performance throughout. When looking for research analysts, most funds target analysts at top-tier bulge-bracket investment banks and want star performers, meaning those in the top bucket for annual bonuses (people in that group know who they are). If you are a top banker in your class, you can expect recruiters to begin contacting you as early as midway through your *first* year.

>
>
> ### Hedge Fund Executive
>
> "We have the pick of the litter, so, on top of everything else, you have to be a 'run-through-the-wall' type of guy. Every person on the sell-side wants to work at a hedge fund, and every person on the buy side wants to work at a hedge fund; at least that's what we think, because there is no lack of candidates for us to look at."

Given the unsystematic nature of hedge fund hiring, we recommend that banking and consulting analysts get ready as early as the middle of the first year of their programs. That means having your resume ready, reading about the industry, learning the different hedge fund styles, practicing your interviewing skills, and monitoring (and, ideally, investing in) the public markets—all the advice we gave in the previous chapter. You may have to find ways to drop what you are doing at work to go on interviews. That may be uncomfortable, but it will be a necessary part of your search, because if you're not willing to do it you can bet someone else is.

We recommend working through the same peer network that helped you get your current position. You should also get in good with your superiors, as they may have relationships with hedge funds and may often be called and asked, "Who are your best people?" You want to be on that list.

Whereas hedge funds used to almost exclusively hire for immediate start dates, meaning analysts were forced to leave their banking programs early, many funds are now hiring for future start dates. That means a hedge fund may lock in a candidate for a start date 12 to 18 months into the future when the banking programs ends. As someone interviewing for a position, you should know at the outset if the fund is open to a flexible start date or would expect you to begin work almost immediately. Maybe you don't want to leave your program early. If leaving early is out of the question, then our advice would be to tell the fund before you get far into the interview process and not string them along. In our opinion, staying in your program for a year is a bare minimum. In fact, most funds will not want to meet you until you've completed a full year, or close to it. The thinking is that you cannot learn enough in less than a year to help a hedge fund, and the fund will not take the time to train you in financial modeling and so on.

BEING IN THE RIGHT GROUP

We have found that hedge funds target candidates from specific banking groups depending on their investment style. For example, there is a definite preference for analysts in groups such as M&A, leveraged finance, financial sponsors, and corporate finance, as they are typically the ones that involve detailed financial modeling, discounted cash flow (DCF) analysis, and accounting and balance sheet work. A fund that invests in CDOs, CLOs, or distressed debt is going to prefer someone from high-yield or leveraged finance. Candidates from these groups usually have the skills to go into a value-oriented or stock-picking hedge fund—whether that is event-driven, long/short, or fundamental value.

Some of the larger hedge funds may have separate industry groups. In such a fund there may be a health care portfolio manager, a senior analyst, and a junior analyst. If you are in an industry-specific group such as health care, biotechnology, energy, financial services, metals and mining, or telecom/technology, you could be attractive to a

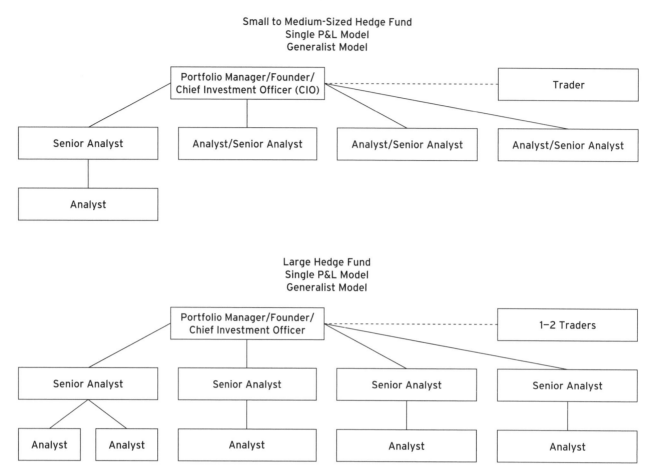

Figure 3.1 Organizational Charts: Single P&L Model

fund that has that same focus. If you have an undergraduate degree in biotechnology or premed or have some science degree and then worked in a healthcare group at an investment bank, you may be in a stronger position than a generalist analyst to get a position as a junior healthcare analyst at a hedge fund that is organized by industry type. (See Figure 3.1 for a single P&L model organizational chart.)

TRADERS

As we've stated earlier, one of the misconceptions about hedge funds is that they are all the same—namely, active trading firms that take short-term positions in a variety of securities. Most hedge funds are in fact long-term equity investors, and, while they have in-house traders, they do not have much of a need for day traders who have worked at proprietary trading firms. Those individuals are used to moving in and out of positions at a furious pace and making their own decisions. Most hedge funds have portfolio managers and investment professionals who are making those decisions and are therefore not looking for traders to do the investing. Instead, they seek execution traders to put on and take off the positions and to help monitor Wall Street news in the portfolio's positions.

Glocap Insight	We have been told by some hedge funds that they can't hire someone who has never bought a stock in his or her life. Others don't care as much, with the thinking being that as a junior hire the individual will not be picking stocks on their first day at work.

The majority of hedge funds want execution traders who can come in and complete a trade, and thus, from our experience, most traders brought on at the junior level are execution traders. These are not people who come in with ideas and have their own accounts. As you will see in Case Study 6 later in the chapter, the sales and trading programs (be it fixed income or equity) are good training grounds for traders. Equity or debt capital markets also provide exposure to the markets and can be good feeders into a trading position. At a more senior level, traders who have worked on the proprietary trading desks at investment banks would be desirable, as these desks function in a very similar way to hedge funds. Although many traders are content-executing trades, we have seen junior traders groomed into more value-added traders.

For the more trading-oriented hedge funds there may be more opportunities for sell-side traders, as they have experience trading based on information flow and momentum. Sell-side traders, such as those in investment banks, are historically in that flow of information, making them more valuable to a hedge fund.

OUT OF PRIVATE EQUITY

A new trend that we have seen developing recently is hedge funds hiring out of private equity funds (see Case Study 8). These individuals have typically completed investment banking or consulting programs and are in the middle of a two- to three-year stint at a private equity fund. Instead of continuing on the traditional path to a career in private equity—which would mean going on to business school and then reentering private equity once they have their MBAs—we've seen these pre-MBA analysts making themselves available to hedge funds, which see them as more seasoned investors than those straight out of banking programs. This is particularly true with long/short fundamental equity shops, which value the ability to thoroughly analyze potential investments. In general, hedge funds put less of a premium on MBAs than do LBO funds, meaning a candidate who has done his/her two years in a bank or consulting firm and two years at an LBO shop can join a hedge fund and be on a career track without first getting an MBA.

CONSULTING

Some consulting firms have corporate finance groups—these can also be good feeders into hedge funds. If you are in a consulting program, it is imperative that while you are there you keep up with the markets and invest on your own. While some funds will be open to consultants, they will still want to see a solid understanding of finance and investing. As the person did in Case Study 5, we suggest you do what you can to learn finance as well as emphasize how your style of strategic thinking can work in a hedge fund setting.

 **Glocap Insight**   Our advice to those currently in private equity shops or consulting firms is not different from what we tell investment banking analysts: invest on your own, follow the markets, know the different investment styles, and know what you bring to the table.

CASE STUDIES

To follow are several case studies of people who got into hedge funds at the pre-MBA level (remember that grouping doesn't mean they are destined to attend business school). The first four are of people who came out of banking programs and got an analyst position at a hedge fund. We also have an example of someone who made it into hedge funds with a consulting background. There are two stories of individuals who became traders, and one of someone who got in with a private equity background. Some of these people permitted us to reprint their resumes, and they can be found in Appendix B. As you read these case studies and review the resumes, take note of the candidates' backgrounds, what they studied, and how they prepared for their entrance into hedge funds. We also recommend paying careful attention to the description that each gives about the interview(s). In addition to outlining the process, many of these former candidates in whose footsteps you want to follow give specific details about the questions they were asked and the scenarios they were presented.

Case Study 1: Bulge-Bracket Banker Lands at a Distressed Debt Fund

This person comes from a more diverse background but was able to get into a distressed debt fund. Although he did not major in finance as an undergraduate, he made good use of his summers and that helped him get into a top analyst training program.

■ ■ ■

I came from a varied background (not purely finance), which, I believe, helped me in the end, but made me a little nervous along the way. I graduated from an Ivy League school in 2005 with a major in public policy. At first I was a biology major, but after I had done two years of premed course work, I realized I had no desire to be a doctor. I had taken a lot of math in high school and some economics courses. I continued with both in college even while I was premed, and found that I particularly enjoyed economics.

After my sophomore year I stayed on campus and did economics research for a professor. At the time I was thinking maybe I'd get a PhD in the subject, since I enjoyed coming up with theory and seeing if it worked out in the real world. However, I quickly learned that life as a professor can be a grind, where you aren't always able to sit around and theorize all day with unlimited resources, and, frankly, most research wasn't necessarily all that fun. It was at that point that I noticed a number of my friends were going into investment banking.

After learning about banking through some daylong seminars I attended during the winter of my junior year, I tried to get a summer analyst position at an investment bank, but, despite making it to a few final rounds, came up empty-handed. I remember being asked if I had taken any finance or accounting courses. Unfortunately for me, the answer to both questions was no. Instead, I landed a summer financial analyst position at a major automotive company. I have always loved cars, and it was a great summer, but working there also convinced me that I didn't want to pursue a traditional corporate finance position. My friends who had gotten summer investment banking jobs seemed to be doing more exciting things, and it seemed like they had greater commitment to their work.

Luckily for me, the summer post I did get paved the way for me to get into an analyst program at a top-tier investment bank after graduation. In fact, I was accepted to more than one program and chose one that was group-specific and got me into the mergers and acquisitions (M&A) group. I consider myself very quantitative and M&A seemed tailored to that strength; I also knew it would give me a lot of options if I wanted to leave investment banking, as M&A analysts are the most highly recruited analysts out of i-banking analyst programs.

Even though I liked investing (I had been trading on my own during school and continued to do so a bit during my analyst program), I didn't know much about hedge funds. That soon changed as I saw the second-year analysts in my program going to private equity and hedge funds. My intrigue about hedge funds grew as I started to get the sense that the people on the buy-side (my bank's clients) were the ones making decisions that mattered. As a banker you're not putting your money on the table; rather, you're trying to get your models done as quickly as possible because the client needs them. As an investor you're more on the line, and I loved the idea of taking risk and being rewarded for good ideas and decisions. Now, I had the impetus I needed to learn about the different hedge fund styles and figure out what my skills were good for.

I began to think about leaving my program in February of my first year as an analyst. A friend of mine who was also a first-year analyst had left to join a macro hedge fund around that time, and I saw there were opportunities out there and there was no reason to wait. I ruled out large-cap private equity because I felt the first two years at a big PE shop would be mostly grunt work, and then I would be spit out and have to go to business school. I had taken tons of finance and accounting my senior year, business school–level classes to make up for my initial deficiency, and saw no reason to go back to school and take the same courses over again.

I also noticed a distinct difference between the culture of a PE fund and that of a hedge fund. I got the sense that many PE firms were the types of places that could have a few guys and each would be in a separate office, whereas a typical hedge fund may have 20 people all sitting together on a trading floor. It was like comparing a team in a locker room at halftime, figuring out how to improve upon their first half, to a bunch of guys who all wanted to be the coach and analyze plays on their own. I liked the collegial atmosphere of hedge funds, and it made a lot more sense to me. The office environment of many PE funds eerily reminded me of the closed-doors world of banking again.

My first order of business was to explore the different hedge fund strategies. After that it was a simple process, as recruiters tend to approach analysts in banking programs. They would ask if I wanted to come in for an interview. I always said yes, since I wanted to give myself the widest possible net to find opportunities. Once I met them, they would ask if I was interested in PE or hedge funds. I told them I was open to PE but preferred hedge funds, and I made sure to have reasons to give them. In addition to the collegial nature of hedge funds, I said I liked that hedge funds had the ability to take short- or long-term positions without constraints. I found that having a specific answer to the "Why a hedge fund?" question was important and knew that I should not be wishy-washy. My philosophy is you've got to know what you want and then you have to say it firmly. Don't just say you want hedge funds—say you want X type of hedge fund and explain why you have the skills for that style. In my case I had zeroed in on distressed debt and was able to show that my mathematical background and my experience doing due diligence on and performing financial modeling for potential investments made me suited for that style.

I interviewed at several different funds—some big ones (more than $2 billion in AUM) and some not so big ones (less than $1 billion in AUM). At first the process was pretty daunting and I didn't make it past the first rounds. One place was a long/short shop and they asked for a ton of investment ideas. I had some, but was working 100-hour weeks and didn't have as many as they wanted. Still, it was a learning experience and helped me with my other interviews.

The interview process at the firm where I am now began with a super Saturday. About 100 candidates were brought in. We rotated out of a single conference room into one of two offices and were interviewed for about 30 minutes each. One thing I can say about my experience interviewing for a hedge fund versus the interviews I had had for an i-bank about a year earlier is that I felt more confident. After all, I had come from one of the most quantitative groups on the Street and felt that my modeling abilities and knowledge of how to look at investments were as good as any other candidate's, in contrast to when I was coming from a nonfinance background in college and interviewing for finance jobs against finance and business majors.

During the first 20 minutes at the hedge fund, my interviewer, a partner with whom I now work closely, focused on getting to know me and I was not asked a single finance question. Rather, he asked things like: What school did you go to? Did you like it? What activities did you do there? Did you like your investment bank? Why are you leaving? (It would not be a good idea to answer that by saying you didn't like working 100 hours a week or because you wanted to make more money.) Are you a social person? What do you do on the weekends? Like many other interviewers, he asked me about some of my more interesting hobbies and things that we had in common (for instance, we both really like hockey).

The last 10 minutes were when he asked for investment ideas. You must be prepared with a view. The people interviewing you want to see your thoughts and logic. They may challenge your assumptions, so it's important to keep your cool. And, if they point out something to you that you didn't know, it's okay to say something like "I never thought of it that way," but try to make this new idea align with your overall viewpoint. I always had one trading idea ready that I knew inside and out and also two backups that I could speak about. For the first I could rattle off historical revenue and earnings before interest, taxes, depreciation, and amortization (EBITDA) figures for three years and my investment's macroeconomic drivers. I knew what was going on in my company, its industry, and its competitors, and any major changes that had occurred in the past couple of years. I could speak about whether the company was in or near bankruptcy (this was a distressed debt fund, after all). For my backup ideas I would make sure to pick companies in different industries in case my interviewer didn't know my company's business well.

"My philosophy is you've got to know what you want and then you have to say it firmly. Don't just say you want hedge funds—say you want X type of hedge fund and explain why you have the skills for that style."

On the Monday or Tuesday after super Saturday the recruiters with whom I was working told me the hedge fund wanted me to come back for a second round. This round happened a week or two later. Basically, they wanted me to meet everyone at the firm, so in this round I met about seven people. Some asked only personality questions and others focused on finance ones. Needless to say, the sheer amount of interviews was pretty grueling.

I had made a point during the first round to ask about the entire process so nothing would take me by surprise. That's how I knew the last round would include a financial modeling test. About five of us from the first group of about 100 candidates were brought back for a third round, and I knew I was close to an offer. For the exam I was given a company, had to download financial statements from Capital IQ, and then had to do a full model with the three major statements—the income statement, cash flow statement, and balance sheet. I was told to take as long as I needed and was done in two hours—and that included some mini interviews from people who came in while

I was modeling. After my work was checked, I was interviewed some more by the senior analyst I currently work with the most, and then I met the founder of the firm for about 20 minutes. After I spoke to the founder, the senior analyst voiced some concerns about me. Specifically, he said that coming from banking they were concerned I might not be ready to be an investor and take risk. I answered that I had traded both during school and while I had been a banking analyst (for less than a year). I'd had success and failure trading in the past and could point to that as my ability to be an investor and take risk.

I didn't get much flak for leaving my banking program early, since my former group adheres to the "two years and out . . . at the most" banking principle, and doesn't promote very many analysts to the associate level. And there was not much the bank could do to counter anyway since I had already signed a contract with the hedge fund.

Going through the process the way I did, I would say that if you definitely want to work in a hedge fund you should find out what you're good at, what you like, and pursue that. If you want to do distressed debt, then you should go into your recruiter interview and say you want to do it and give good reasons why. After all, you want to work in an environment where you fit in and enjoy what you do, or else you can never really be successful or happy.

See Resume A in Appendix B on page 163.

Case Study 2: Getting In from a Second-Tier Bank

Here is an example of someone who got a position as a hedge fund analyst coming out of a second-tier bank. While in his analyst program he applied himself, read about investing, and created a mock portfolio. He first encountered hedge funds through a summer position.

■ ■ ■

I got a taste for hedge funds through an internship during the summer before my senior year of college. I was fortunate to get the interview for this position through some personal contacts I had. This was a small fund with a niche focus investing in small-cap high-yield bonds and distressed debt. If I had wanted to come back and work at this fund after graduation they probably would have hired me, but honestly, I don't think I would have been ready to work full-time at a hedge fund. As an intern I was fine, but I thought I would be better off getting banking experience.

I graduated from an Ivy League university in 2005 with a degree in political science. I also took some economics courses. When I got back to school for my senior year I focused on investment banking programs. Given that I took very little finance in school, the fact that I did a summer at a hedge fund helped me get into a banking program, as they all want to see some interest in finance—be it from course work or internships.

Although I wasn't in a bulge-bracket program, I felt my bank was up-and-coming and had a strong leveraged finance group. In my program (and I suspect with most others) the learning curve was weighted toward the first six months of the program.

Since the finance was new to me, I benefited from working on deals, learning to model, helping to draft the screening and leverage finance memos, and going on road shows.

In my free time I dedicated myself to following stocks and learning as much about the philosophy of investing as I could. In addition to reading *Security Analysis* by Benjamin Graham and David Dodd, *The Intelligent Investor* by Benjamin Graham, *You Can Be a Stock Market Genius* by Joel Greenblatt, and strategy papers of Michael Mauboussin (the head strategist at Legg Mason), I read investing/market blogs and any articles and research papers I could find. I had invested on my own in college, but was restricted from doing much during my analyst program. I knew that it would be important to have something to talk about during interviews, so I created a mock portfolio and followed the market. Having that portfolio along with an understanding of different investing strategies allowed me to ask better questions during interviews. Otherwise, you end up sounding like an investment banker who just likes to model.

> *"In my free time I dedicated myself to following stocks and learning as much about the philosophy of investing as I could."*

I was contacted by headhunters about 10 months into the first year of my analyst program and went on my first interview early in the summer. Although I had my sights set on hedge funds, I went on some private equity interviews as well. I liked that hedge fund investing allowed for more freedom—you can short a company that you don't like, buy puts or calls, and so on. In private equity, it seemed that if you like a company, you have to bid against other funds. If stocks are expensive then you have to either do a bad deal or sit around and wait for the markets to improve. Within hedge funds I focused my attention on funds that did value investing, special situations, and/or high-yield instruments. These were the styles that appealed to me once I had done my research and to which I thought my background was best suited.

The first rounds of most interviews were usually pretty informal, with some finance questions mixed in (if you were required to bring a stock pick or take a test, they usually informed you ahead of time so you could prepare). I was always asked why I was interested in hedge funds and why I wanted to work at the particular fund where I was being interviewed. Sometimes first-round interviews can get a little more complex. During the first round at one fund I was given two investment options; one had an IRR (internal rate of return) of 20% and the other had an IRR of 30%. I was asked if there was any reason not to invest in the one with the higher IRR. In this case, the fund wanted me to understand what IRR meant at a deeper level and to know that a lot depends on how much you can invest and how long you can keep it invested. I was often asked what my weaknesses were (and each time was told not to say that I work too hard).

The next rounds got more specific in terms of the deals I worked on and were also when I got the proverbial case studies, was asked for investment ideas, and got some brainteasers. Several funds required written case studies for a second round. At one fund I was given a case study in which I was told to evaluate a company and choose where to invest. The company had three tranches of debt as well as equity.

I had to write up my answer, and that's how it was determined who got to the final round. In the final round I was asked more questions about my answer.

Overall, there is very little standardization among questions asked during hedge fund interviews. I've been asked everything under the sun. I'd say it's important to know the various hedge fund styles and which suits your background. If you go into an interview and are not interested in or knowledgeable about what the fund invests in, your interviewer will see it and pick up on it, meaning if you're interested in equities and find yourself interviewing at a fund that specializes in debt, your interviewer will pick up on your ambivalence and lack of knowledge about the fund.

The fund where I am working now is a smaller value-focused/special situations shop that will also invest in some high-yield instruments. This fund's style meshes perfectly with my interests and I was prepared with lots of questions about the fund's strategy. At one point I asked my interviewer (the head of research) if he had read Greenblatt's book, as it seemed to pertain to the fund's strategy. Ironically, he told me he was going to require whoever got the job to read it, so I scored some points and made a good impression. During the second round at this fund I met with the partners, who asked me some technical accounting questions. They also asked what I thought about the market and what stocks I followed. The final round was a written test that asked accounting questions and for my opinions on a specific company, based on the financial statements provided. I found the test pretty fair and doable compared to ones I had taken during other interviews. None of the questions were too crazy and there were no brainteasers.

I got an offer in November of my second year, left my analyst program, and began my hedge fund career. I didn't get much flak for leaving my program early. Most people just wished me luck. Since I was not in a bulge-bracket training program, I faced a little more of an uphill battle and may not have gotten some of the same opportunities as if, say, I was coming out of a Goldman Sachs. If I had been at one of those firms, the funds might not have cared what stocks I followed.

My advice to those interested in hedge funds would be to find out what type of hedge fund style is best for you. Most funds will ask why you want to do this type of investing, so your answer had better be convincing. Read as much as you can. If you are applying to an equity shop, then you must have a list of stocks that you follow, that you have invested in, and that you can talk about. You will be asked your opinion, so you have to have one. The banking programs provide very useful skills, but extra work has to be done to be prepared for many hedge fund interviews (especially equity funds).

See Resume B in Appendix B on page 164.

Case Study 3: Making It with a Liberal Arts Degree

This person only had limited exposure to finance before getting into a boutique investment banking program. What he did have, however, were an aggressive attitude, an insatiable appetite for reading, and an enjoyment of investing on his own.

■ ■ ■

Coming from a liberal arts background, I was at a disadvantage in getting into finance and pursuing a career on Wall Street. Although I graduated with an Ivy League degree (class of 2005), I had taken no finance and had very little exposure to accounting. My curiosity about finance began to take shape during my sophomore year when I became friendly with a group of students who were very familiar with and knew from an early age that they wanted to work on Wall Street. These friends of mine seemed to know all about the intricacies of the world of finance and Wall Street in general. They knew which banks and private equity funds they would work for and how their finance careers would evolve. I knew none of that and had never actively followed the stock market. Being around these friends, I grew curious as to what they were talking about. An avid reader, I grabbed the closest copy of Benjamin Graham's *The Intelligent Investor* and read it thoroughly. This was my introduction to investing and finance in general, and it helped open my eyes and spark my interest in investing.

Despite my newfound interest in finance and Wall Street, I had a hard time getting an appropriate investment banking summer internship after my junior year. It didn't help that my previous summer I had a nonfinance position with a non-governmental organization (NGO) and I had taken no finance courses whatsoever. In fact, I was denied by every firm I applied to except one bank that saw I had a genuine interest in the public markets and was able to look past my lack of finance and accounting experience. I was placed in the equity capital markets group, which was great because I got a real introduction to the markets and how they operate, but on a practical level it was not a place to acquire the tools necessary for a career in finance.

Completing my banking internship made me realize that I needed a work environment where I would acquire and hone the corporate finance skills I lacked in a short period of time. When I returned to school for my senior year I focused my efforts on getting into an analyst training program at a smaller boutique M&A and restructuring shop. Since small shops are known for giving more responsibility to analysts, I felt I would have to force myself to learn what I needed to know. I was successful in landing a position in a New York-based boutique and was able to learn finance, accounting, and modeling. I also began investing on my own while I was in the program. I didn't put down large sums of money, since I didn't have any, but I found I enjoyed the process of seeking out companies and discovering absolute value or a possible short.

Once recruiting season came around at the end of my first year, it seemed that everyone in my banking program wanted to go into private equity, and it didn't take long for recruiters to begin calling. I began my program in July 2005, and I'd say recruiters started calling around May of 2006, not even a year into my program. With all the recruiters pushing private equity and hedge funds, I made it a point to learn as much about each as possible. I read *Barbarians at the Gate, Liar's Poker, When Genius Failed,* Benjamin Graham's *Security Analysis,* Peter Lynch's *Beating the Street,* excerpts from Warren Buffett's annual letters to his shareholders, and George Soros' *The Alchemy of Finance.* The more I read, the more I realized that private equity was not for me. I wasn't interested in the process of using tons of leverage to buy businesses and enter the institutional world of private equity. Private equity, like banking, is very structured, and it seems like everyone does their two years, then they go to business school, and then they return to the PE shop they left. I wanted to invest in the public markets and have the opportunity to be more entrepreneurial. I wanted to gain the skills that would allow me to eventually invest on my own, and I felt being at a hedge fund would pave the way for me to do that.

I told the recruiters that I only wanted to target multi-strategy hedge funds because it was too early in my career to begin specializing in one specific strategy. I made sure each fund had both a credit and an equity focus in order to ensure exposure to both. Unfortunately, I completely bombed my first interview—mainly because I was unprepared. I remember being asked: "In your daily life, where do you find value?" I had absolutely no answer, which was extremely frustrating. I had never thought that way before. After reflecting on the interview, I realized they wanted to know where I found value in everyday items like the price of lunch, rent for my apartment, and so on. That line of questioning made me look more deeply at my own thought process, and the experience helped me prepare for subsequent interviews. Again, I read more—*Trading to Win* by Ari Kiev and *Learn to Earn* by Peter Lynch. To refine my thought process I also started to apply what I was reading in my daily life. I began thinking more about where I found value. What everyday items did I buy, and which did I choose not to buy? Did I take a taxi, and why or why not? Thinking about things in this way helped my own investing and prepared me for other interviews. More than just seeing that you have invested, hedge funds want to see that you're *interested* in investing and that you have a thought process with regard to the positions you take.

In all my interviews I was asked if I invested and what the *motivation* behind my investments was. Was I putting money to work just because I had too much in savings or because my dad had told me to put some money in a mutual fund? Were there other reasons? Of course, they wanted to hear that I was truly interested in the markets and finding undervalued companies. I got into a debate at one interview when I told them I had a personal investment and was bullish on a company the fund had shorted. They couldn't believe my reasons for why the stock was undervalued and the debate became pretty heated, but I held my ground. (Note: The stock has gone up 20% since I interviewed with them.)

Once I answered the "Do you invest?" question positively, my interviewers would typically jump right in and bombard me with questions about my analysis and the specifics of each investment. What do you invest in? Why did you buy that stock? Where is it trading? At what price did you buy it? What do the horizons look like for the next five years? What is your price target? It seemed like the more answers I had to their questions, the more questions there were and the more deeply they probed into my answers.

All together I interviewed at five to seven places and had my share of technical and personal/fit type questions. Some of the technical questions were case studies.

In one, I was given two hours to examine the financials of a company and told to pretend I owned every part of its capital structure. I was then asked what I would do with the different securities of the company and the company itself. I hadn't worked much with bank debt and couldn't come back to them with a specific decision on what I would do with this company's debt or its convertible bonds.

Ironically, the fund that eventually extended me an offer focused mostly on personality questions. I remember being asked: What's your favorite movie? What music do you like? Where did you grow up? What do your parents do? How did that affect your personality? Why did you write what you wrote (for a senior thesis)? How do you define whether something is expensive? I met everyone at this firm, from the head of investor relations to one of the secretaries. The technical questions and brainteasers came later once it was apparent there was a personality fit. They asked me to walk them through an LBO and dissect a company's financial statements. They asked my opinion of a company I had never heard of before. I knew they wanted to find out how I thought and formulated my investment ideas. I'd say 90% of the hedge funds out there are looking to see how people analyze problems and show they can approach a situation from both a micro and a macro level.

The whole interview process can be pretty overwhelming, grueling, and frustrating. At almost every interview I had I was forced to think in new ways that were completely alien to me. Although this was frustrating, I realized that being a professional investor forces one to continuously think in novel ways, and in order to succeed in an environment like that, one has to be flexible and innovative in one's thought process. Until I realized this and was comfortable with it, the interview process seemed like it was going to last forever.

> "Although this was frustrating, I realized that being a professional investor forces one to continuously think in novel ways, and in order to succeed in an environment like that, one has to be flexible and innovative in one's thought process."

I began interviewing at the firm that eventually extended me an offer in June, and got an offer in late September. You have to do all of this at the same time you are working 110-hour weeks at your investment bank, which presents interesting conflicts. At the beginning of the process I had to invent a lot of reasons why I was leaving the office (there were a whole lot of doctor appointments and my sister came to town a few times). As the processes dragged on it became harder to lie to my supervisors.

Luckily for me, the firm at which I got an offer is an exception to the norm that hedge funds demand you drop out of your banking program early. At a specific point I had to tell my managing directors that I didn't plan to come back for a third year and was looking for a new job, but they gave me references once I told them that I was focusing on a position that would start the summer after I completed my two-year commitment. Leaving a banking program early may be good for some (it gets them into the hedge fund of their choice), but not as beneficial to others who feel they have more to learn. In my case, I was fortunate that the partner at the hedge fund thought I would get a lot out of the final year of my program, so I didn't have to worry about burning any bridges, which was my main concern. He felt that if I stayed longer I would be put on more complicated deals and that would benefit his fund in the long run.

I was successful in landing my current position because I believe I showed a genuine interest in the public markets and investing in general. Especially after my first interview, I tried to be extremely thorough and complete in my preparation for the interviews; I would try to anticipate all the questions they could ask me about my investments and my investment theses. It's also important to remember in applying for these jobs that personal fit is an important component because the vast majority of hedge funds are very small shops. In a place where there are few people responsible for investing vast sums of money, getting along with your co-workers and inducing a positive working environment are very important.

If seniors in college came to me today and said they wanted to work at a hedge fund, I would ask why. If their motivation is to be a multimillionaire when they hit 30, then I would tell them they are doomed to fail. I would ask if they invest. If the answer to that is no, I would also ask, why not? If you really think hedge funds are for you, then you should start investing and read about investing. In my case, I like looking for value; that makes me excited, and it has to turn you on as well. For many people who work at hedge funds, investing was a hobby that turned into a profession. Sure, you do a lot of technical analysis, but at the end of the day you have to decide if you are going to put money into a specific investment or not and you have to have a thoroughly thought- out investment thesis as to why you want to take a particular position.

See Resume C in Appendix B on page 165.

Case Study 4: A Typical Banking Hire

This candidate came from a strong finance background, had the appropriate summer jobs during college, got into a top banking program, and stayed there for three years. He networked his way into a hedge fund interview, but after that he was scrutinized as any other candidate would be.

■ ■ ■

I came out of a fairly typical background—Ivy League undergraduate degree in finance—and broke into hedge funds in 2003. At that time hedge funds were not as popular an option as they are today. Now, I know it's very competitive to get in and there is more of an emphasis on prior investing experience. Fortunately, I got in without too much hands-on investing.

My two summer jobs during college—working at a brokerage firm after my sophomore year and as a summer analyst in an investment bank in Asia following my junior year—helped pave the way for my first job after graduating. Leading up to my graduation in 2000 I interviewed at investment banks and top-tier consulting firms. I wasn't even thinking about hedge funds. At the time everyone wanted to do banking, and I followed suit, landing a spot in an analyst training program at a New York–based investment bank.

I was fortunate that going into the program I knew I wanted to be in the M&A group and I got what I wanted. Since I had studied finance, my aim was to work in a group that would allow me to put some of the things I had learned into practice, such as building models. I also knew I wanted to work on live deals. Without an industry preference I didn't mind being a generalist.

I stayed in the M&A group for two years and then switched to the industrial group for the third. I thought it would be a good chance to learn more about capital raising and high-yield debt issuance. Finally, after three years of banking I wanted to move on. I found banking to be a very client-driven culture and thought I would be stuck doing what clients wanted. I was more interested in doing analysis from a decision maker's perspective.

My job search was broad-based and unstructured and included looking at private equity and corporate development positions. Eventually my networking paid off, as a friend of mine put me in touch with the partner/head trader of a small risk arbitrage/event-driven hedge fund with whom he had studied. Although I had gotten in the door, I still had to go through a lengthy interview process. This fund was looking for a junior trader, but after meeting me they thought I could be an analyst.

My first discussion with the partner was a simple conversation. He asked if I invested in stocks, and I had to respond that I basically had zero investing experience on a professional level and very little on a personal level. I told him that I was restricted from investing in companies that I knew well and that I didn't have enough money to invest in others. I knew that my lack of investing probably didn't help me, but it was the truth. On a scale of 1 to 100 (100 being the highest), I was probably a 25 to 30 in terms of being passionate about the markets. Nevertheless, the fund was looking for a fairly junior analyst out of a banking program and I fit that bill.

In addition to meeting the partner, I met three other people. I was asked why I was interested in hedge funds and not private equity. My answer was that I didn't want to sit at a firm for three years working on one deal. I knew the investment evaluation processes of hedge funds and private equity funds were much different and preferred the former.

During the second round of interviews I met with the fund's portfolio manager, and it was apparent that he was looking to see if there was a personality fit. You can't get around the fact that if the people at a fund don't like you they won't hire you. In addition to judging whether they liked me, I think the people I met were trying to determine if I could learn their style of investing. No one really does risk arbitrage in a training program, so if you join such a fund the people there know they are going to have to teach you that style. They want to know that you are smart enough to absorb things quickly. My background seemed well suited to risk arb—I could build models, had done deals, had good financial statement analysis skills, and was a generalist. I know now that a lot of the value in risk arbitrage/event-driven investing is the ability to assess a situation quickly. You have to be able to take a view of a given event. Everyone is racing and trying to arrive at an answer while at the same time the stock price is moving. I used this round of interviews to ask questions about the firm—just like a good investor will have questions for a company, I had a list of questions to ask my interviewers, and they liked my curiosity. Before going on my first interview I Googled risk arbitrage/event-driven hedge funds and learned as much as I could. When they asked me if I knew what the style was, I was able to give the short, textbook answer, and I was able to tell them that I wanted to learn more about it.

The third round of interviews was when I was given a case study. I was presented with a situation, something like: Here's company X; a well-known investor is proposing to buy company X and merge it with one of his other holdings. I was told to take a look at the stock price and, using the financials, give my view on company X's valuation. This exercise took half a day and was done in the fund's offices.

I was left in the lurch for about a month before I was asked to come back for some more interviews. I was then given two more case studies, which took the better part of a day to finish. I didn't mind doing these, knowing they wanted to see that I knew what drove stock prices. I guess I met their expectations, because I got an offer.

I was fortunate enough to interview with easygoing people, so although you get a little nervous during any interviews, for me it was a fairly smooth process. My advice to those interested in hedge funds in today's hiring environment would be to learn the various hedge fund styles. There's a valuation component at the core of every strategy, so learning that is paramount.

See Resume D in Appendix B on page 166.

Case Study 5: A Consultant Gets In

When this person's visions of using his math skills to join a quantitative fund faded, he took the unusual step of going into consulting and still got into a hedge fund.

■ ■ ■

I may have been different from other hedge fund candidates in that I decided somewhat early on—first or second year in college—that I was pretty sure that I wanted to work at a hedge fund. I was always into math, and a quant fund sounded like it would be a fascinating, potentially lucrative direction to take. I did what I could to position myself for this but encountered a couple of obstacles along the way—first, none of my professors had faith in quant-based trading, and second, by the time I graduated I was more interested in leading a business than in statistics-based arbitrage. I graduated in 2004, though, at the top of my class with a degree in mathematics from a West Coast college.

On graduating, I took a job in the San Francisco office of a leading strategy consulting company. Consulting was great and I learned quite a bit, but I needed something more than that and did almost everything I could to position myself for a role that would better fit my personality and ambitions. Private equity had its allure and I knew that it was hard to get in from consulting, but I tried to give it a go anyway.

From my perspective, people working at private equity funds didn't have to deal with the mundane tasks of consulting (ugh, PowerPoint slides!), and they were investing with and earning real money.

I gave myself an intensive course in finance. This was in addition to the 60 to 70 hours a week I spent at my consulting job. It was intense; I threw away my social life for the better part of a year. It was a little demoralizing when the private equity recruiting process came and went without my getting an offer from any of the big shops with which I had interviewed, but in retrospect the results of the recruiting process made complete sense. I tend to be a contrarian, I question a lot, and I have never had great respect for authority—I think there is clearly a private equity attitude and I certainly did not have it. Coming from technical roots, I didn't want business school to be my only ticket up. In addition, I saw that the career trajectory in private equity seemed, to me at least, to be too slow and definitely not fitting my personality or long-term career goals.

I was working with a recruiter who had been trying to get me to interview with this one hedge fund for months but I had kept putting her off—I didn't know much about the fund and was still set on completing the next $20 billion LBO deal. I finally capitulated and agreed to interview with them.

This fund (I later learned) takes a fundamental/value-based approach to public and private investments. I began trading stocks on my own when I was 10 years old. It wasn't very sophisticated investing, but I understood the markets and grew to enjoy investing. The experience of researching companies from an early age made this style of investing attractive to me. Since it was located in another city, my first round of interviews was over the telephone. I was given some logic problems and we talked about stocks—I was asked to name a few companies in which I would consider investing or not and to explain why. I was also asked a lot of corporate finance questions. That part was pretty intense. I told them I had studied by myself and I think they wanted to see how I did, because they were asking me stuff that no consultant in his or her right mind should know.

I did some research before the on-site interview and found out more about this fund. The more I discovered, the more interested I became. Once I was there they grilled me for about an hour on corporate finance and then they gave me an IQ test. I think they wanted to see how I was under pressure, because they just printed something off the Internet and gave me 10 minutes to complete it on the spot. I found my interviewers to be very nice and very intellectual and I felt very comfortable. Another person asked me about books I had read, and he had read every one I mentioned—even the autobiography of an obscure mathematician. We also talked about some financial mathematics and option pricing that I didn't know too well. I wasn't asked about my consulting, but I was given a modeling test. I think they were a little surprised at how slow I was at modeling out a cash flow statement compared to a banking candidate, but I did it.

On the personal side, I was asked what books I read and to name a few of my favorites. I'm an avid reader, but I didn't have any answers prepared so I think my responses came out as very honest. I was asked if I wanted to live where this fund was located and I said I would consider it.

I didn't get much feedback during or right after my interview. A couple of days later the firm called with some follow-up questions and to see if I was sincere about moving to their city. It took a month before I finally got the offer. They checked with, literally, eight of my references. Before accepting I had them fly me back to their offices so I could get a final feel for the firm.

It wasn't until I took the offer that I found out the group I was interviewing with was a large part of one of the biggest hedge funds out there. My job there is amazing— I have more responsibility than I ever thought would have been possible with my level of experience. I couldn't have imagined a better place to work. All the work I had done to teach myself finance had definitely paid off.

Everyone else who works at this fund came out of a banking program, and I was told that the reason they don't normally hire consultants is that consultants typically don't have any idea about finance. I believe I was able to make a case for myself because I knew the theory behind finance and had also taught myself the technical aspects. A lot of bankers know the technical part of finance and are Excel experts, but they don't have the business intuition that consultants do. In my view, and I'm biased, I'd say a consultant who can understand yield curves, do a DCF analysis, and build a cash flow statement is in great shape to be a hedge fund candidate.

> *"People have to understand what each fund does before just saying that they are interested in hedge funds."*

My primary advice to someone aspiring to work at a hedge fund is to work to be at the top of your consulting or investment banking analyst class. Taking the time to invest in public securities will be a major differentiating factor. After that, if you can discuss the rationales of two or three investments you've made, are comfortable with finance, and understand the macro issues affecting the markets, you will be in good shape. At my fund having an undergraduate GPA above 3.7 is a must. We want to see that candidates excel at everything they do, and having a low GPA shows that you either screwed around during college or didn't have the commitment to do well.

I would also advise those interested in hedge funds to make sure they know the industry. I think a lot of candidates have the wrong impression of hedge funds. The biggest misconception is that these are risky, shadowy organizations. My fund is first and foremost a value investor. Our returns will almost always be more stable than the S&P 500 or almost any other equity indexes. We take long/short positions in public stocks and also have positions in private companies. When people ask me, I don't even say I work at a hedge fund. I just say I work at an investment firm. People have to understand what each fund does before just saying that they are interested in hedge funds.

Case Study 6: Breaking into Trading

This person benefited by being in the sales and trading program of a major sell-side firm. He also had buy-side experience, giving him a good perspective of both sides of the trading spectrum.

■ ■ ■

As a trader, I found breaking into hedge funds to be a little different than it would have been had I pursued a research analyst position. I graduated in 2004 from a small liberal arts college on the West Coast with a double major in economics and psychology. While in school I had two internships that introduced me to the world of money management. First, following my sophomore year I interned at a small money manager/financial adviser in my hometown. Then, just prior to my senior year I had an internship at a major West Coast fixed income fund.

In addition to solidifying my interest in investing, the second internship offered me a full-time job, which gave me the luxury of going through my senior year with an offer in hand. I interviewed at several investment banks and ended up with four offers from traditional two- to three-year investment banking or sales and trading analyst programs on the West Coast and one in New York. The advice I received was that if I wanted to forge a career in finance I should start out in New York, so I took that position. The job in New York was an equity sales and trading program, not the typical banking one, and this gave me the training I would need to go into trading.

I started my training program in July 2004 and rotated among different groups. I spent time doing trade modeling, developing commission reports, and learning the language of trading on the floor of the New York Stock Exchange. After about 12 months I began trading my own pad under a senior person at the firm. Although I was happy, I started to send my resume to headhunters, knowing that at the end of the two-year program I would either be promoted to an associate or spend a third year as an analyst. Because I was content I wasn't very aggressive with my search.

I always knew I wanted to go to the buy-side, and that was made even more apparent during my time in the trading program. From my experience, as a sell-side trader you are not adding much fundamental investing value, and for me, as someone who was just executing orders, it seemed the job I was doing wasn't capitalizing on my intellectual capacity and educational background. I knew that private equity funds were drawing more candidates from banking rather than trading programs, so I focused on hedge funds. I believe my experience prepared me to make an easier transition to a hedge fund (I didn't have the valuation background to do research). I was also attracted to hedge funds because of the potential to trade more freely and use different types of trades other than the plain-vanilla ones used by mutual funds.

When it became time to interview, the headhunter with whom I was working sent me to a small multi-strategy fund. This fund had 25 people and I literally had to meet every investment professional at the firm—17 in all. Except for the fact that I ended up going to the fund's Connecticut office seven or eight times, the actual interview process wasn't as difficult as it is for research analysts, who are typically given very in-depth projects that require them to analyze and present a potential investment opportunity to the firm. Although not all of the people with whom I met were ones I currently work with, everyone wanted to see if my personality was one that would fit in with the firm. It felt like a fraternity where everyone has to like you before you are asked to join.

In terms of questions, there were some of the typical brainteasers. I was asked what degrees are in the hour and minute hands of a clock if it is 3:30, and to count by powers of 2. I was also asked the standard questions about myself and hedge funds, but most of all they wanted to know my trading/investment process. I walked them through the process of committing capital to the buy-side. I was never asked to value a company.

"It felt like a fraternity where everyone has to like you before you are asked to join."

Looking back, the overall process was pretty informal. Each time I returned to the office to meet more people I would meet with the COO as well. Along the way I was constantly getting feedback via the headhunter. "Okay, that guy likes you. They want to keep the process going." It went on like that for about a month until I had met everyone.

I agree with the common belief that it's important to spend a couple of years or more at a bulge-bracket investment bank before joining a hedge fund. Those types of firms have the resources to teach you how to trade and learn the business on a macro level. In my case, the fund wanted someone with two to four years of experience. They wanted someone who knew the basics and weren't going to train a neophyte. Now, when I talk with traders on the sell-side they appreciate that I spent time on that side of the business and understand how they work. I do not doubt someone could do this job straight out of college; however, I feel an individual's potential upside career development could be dampened by the lack of experience. If someone does get into a fund out of undergraduate school they will have a totally different type of role.

Case Study 7: Swapping the Sell Side for a Long/Short Fund

This person benefited from his own trading background and knowledge of options to land a trading position.

■ ■ ■

I graduated in 2002 from a small liberal arts college with a double major in economics and computer science and then got a master's degree in economics with a concentration in statistics and finance. I definitely wanted to get into finance and thought that a cosci/econ degree, combined with my highly mathematical background, would be a good match for the new Internet economy.

Following graduation, I had offers for full-time associate positions from a few banks and others from the structured finance divisions of some accounting firms. Nevertheless, I ended up going into an analyst training program even though I was the only one with a master's degree. I liked it because it was a rotational program and gave me exposure to different areas, including derivatives, options, asset management, and capital markets.

I began thinking of my next step practically on the first day of my analyst program and began to focus on hedge funds. I had been trading on my own since my sophomore year in college and had taught myself options. I was able to arrange my schedule so I had enough free time during the later years of school to dedicate the time to some long-term investments as well as actively day trading. Even when I lost money it was a great learning experience and it convinced me that I wanted to trade and manage money.

I began to think hard about a change about a year into my program. At the time I was in the equity-linked origination group and knew that I preferred trading to structuring products. I spoke to the proprietary trading desk at my bank, but they couldn't commit to me so I ventured outside.

My first strategy was to contact headhunters. Then I contacted hedge funds directly. In some cases I was able to go on the web sites, find the job postings, and write an e-mail to the head of human resources. I focused on styles that would suit my background—equity, quant, and derivatives. Finally, a headhunter got in touch with me about a firm that was thinking about starting an options practice.

My initial interview was with the CFO/CIO. Following that I met with four of the investment professionals, including the head trader and the portfolio manager. After that they gave me a project to do. I was told to structure some options trades. When I came back to present the trades I was there for an entire day. I also spent time in a casual setting with the people there, which helped them get to know me better. From start to finish I'd say the process took a few months, and it was pretty exhausting. I ended up starting at the hedge fund one month after I got the offer, which meant leaving my banking program after about 18 months. The bank wanted me to stay on and looked at other possibilities for me, but just couldn't come up with something attractive.

"Without a doubt I'd recommend investing in the markets. I learned more doing that than I did in any class. Being modest and not arrogant is always good."

I'm convinced that my math background and the fact that I had been trading on my own during my banking program helped me. Nevertheless, I wouldn't have gotten the offer if there hadn't been a good fit in terms of personality. I am more of a reserved person and by nature not very loud, and this hedge fund has a very professional atmosphere. There are no high-strung egos as there are in some other funds, and that helped me fit in. I also think that being in the earlier stages of my career helped, because the fund was just starting to get more active in options and I was learning how hedge funds and the investment process worked. I think they thought that we (the fund and I) would evolve together at a reasonable pace.

My advice to would-be hedge fund candidates is to make up your minds about what you want to do. Do you want to trade? Do you want to be a research analyst? When

I was interviewing, most hedge funds were looking for analysts. I'd add that learning derivatives helps a lot, as do, I discovered, rotational programs where you learn about many things. Without a doubt I'd recommend investing in the markets. I learned more doing that than I did in any class. Being modest and not arrogant is always good. Many hedge funds already have strong characters and may not be looking for another. Reading is a must, and keeping on top of the *Economist* and *BusinessWeek* will teach you a lot and show you know what's going on in the world.

See Resume E in Appendix B on page 167.

Case Study 8: Making the Switch from Private Equity

Here's an example of someone who was on the path to a career track position in private equity. He had completed a banking program and was working at a major LBO shop, but joined a hedge fund rather than go to business school.

■ ■ ■

I graduated from college in 2001. At that time I don't think I even knew what a hedge fund was, or for that matter a private equity firm. I was an economics major and had always thought I would eventually pursue some type of career in business. I'd watched many of my older Ivy League acquaintances go off into banking or consulting, and once they came back to campus to recruit for their employers, they pitched their current jobs as a stepping-stone to the next big thing. I followed suit.

To prepare for my life after college, I spent the summer between my sophomore and junior years working for a company in Europe. Eager for some exposure to finance, the next summer I worked on the trading floor of a major Wall Street firm. Even though I wasn't actively trading, I was in a finance environment for the first time and was able to watch and learn a lot. At the end of the summer I was invited to join this bank's sales and trading program after graduation. That was a nice offer to have and took some of the stress off my senior year. I interviewed at other banks, but ended up accepting the offer to return, albeit in the investment banking division. I had met a lot of nice people there and felt I fit in with the culture of the firm. I chose to join the industrials group, where I thought I would be exposed to not only many different types of companies but also each of the banking products (debt, equity, and M&A). Still, this was 2001 and it was a tough time for deal flow. I was busy during my first year really only pitching deals. It wasn't until my second year that activity picked up and I managed to close five or six deals. By working closely with my bank's financial sponsors group, I became involved with several private equity firms advising them on M&A and putting together debt financing packages in support of their buyouts.

After about two and a half years in the analyst program I began to think about moving on, with my first choice being private equity. At the time, hedge funds did very little recruiting out of analyst programs. My bank wasn't quite in the first tier of targets for headhunters, and I don't recall getting any inbound calls from headhunters (the same was true for other analysts in my group). I was in my third year, and fortunately a colleague in our firm's financial sponsors group was willing to help me out. I also contacted 15 to 20 firms on my own with varying degrees of success. Finally I was interviewed and accepted into the telecom and media group of a major LBO fund.

I went into my next job thinking I would stay a couple of years and then go to business school. Unfortunately, I was wait-listed at the only two MBA programs to which I had applied. Being wait-listed forced me to think about what I wanted out of business school (and life afterwards). I began to wonder if I could get a job now similar to what I'd want to do after business school. If I could, why wouldn't I take it?

I enjoyed many of the analytics I'd learned in private equity, although I hadn't done any investing in the public markets on my own or in a professional setting. I came from a large LBO fund where there are many layers of professionals and a good deal of hierarchy and process generally, so I wanted a place where junior people were more directly involved. I worked with three headhunters and told them I was willing to look at small private equity funds that would take me in a post-MBA position. It was also at this point that I began to hear of some hedge funds looking to break into private equity investing.

I began to interview with a few hedge funds, and at first I was turned off by the hard-nosed trading mentality of the three hedge funds at which I interviewed. This could have been isolated to those specific funds, but it stressed to me the importance of finding a place with a good fit for my personality. As a general rule, I had found my original private equity interviews to be relatively technical: Interviewers would typically ask me to walk them through a DCF model, explain how a pay-in-kind (PIK) security works, and answer other private equity/banker types of questions. Hedge fund interviewers tended to ask more nuanced questions, focusing on my opinions regarding specific investments and gauging my ability to present a case for or against a certain company.

At the hedge fund where I eventually got an offer, I went into my interviews expecting more technical questions, but didn't get them. It's possible they assumed that I knew my stuff after two years in private equity at a well-known shop. They focused more on qualitative/fit/personality questions, and the tone throughout was more conversational. For instance, they wanted to know what I liked to do outside of work. Since I was coming from a relatively large team and would be working with only two people at this hedge fund, they asked how I would handle doing my own research and probed my ability to generally be a self-starter. The process overall felt pretty informal.

One difference about this particular fund's interview process was that I was given an hour-long written test during the first round. The test focused on my knowledge of valuation metrics, a couple of technical questions on option math and balance sheet/cash flow workings, and some straightforward logic questions at the end.

The second round consisted of a series of interviews with various people at the firm. These tended to focus on my roles on old deals and how I thought about the particular investment. They also asked what I was looking for out of a job at their firm. Following all this was a case study. I was given the name of a company and told to return in one week with a presentation in memo form of around 10 pages giving my views on investments in the company's debt and equity securities. I originally expected to present my thoughts to a small group of four or five people, so when I returned a week later I was surprised to see the entire firm in the main conference room waiting for me. I think more than anything else in this process, it's important to take a strong view (either positive or negative) on a potential investment—in this case, I held nothing back in telling them the company was troubled.

> *"My advice to those interested in hedge funds is that starting off in a banking program is the most direct route to take."*

After the case study I met with the head of the firm. The first thing he did was turn to the last page of the written test I had taken at the outset of my interviews and point out that I had answered three-quarters of the logic questions incorrectly. He also chided me on my relatively low SAT math scores. Fortunately, I had been on a lot of interviews—both for banking programs and at PE firms—so I was comfortable being asked tough questions (or at least questions designed to be harsh) and had responses ready. At this point, I was slightly worn out by the interview process and not much fazed me. In addition, I had been asked to stay on at my private equity firm and that added to my generally relaxed and confident feelings. I think the head of the firm was looking for a calm and well-reasoned reaction, because pretty soon thereafter he began selling the firm and the position to me.

My advice to those interested in hedge funds is that starting off in a banking program is the most direct route to take. Within banking, there are several options in terms of which groups give you the best experience. My own view is that leveraged finance groups, in which analysts work to present the credit case of a company to a bank, are great places to get modeling experience and learn solid due diligence techniques (and how to think critically when meeting with company management). Once you begin interviewing, you should, of course, have a couple of good investment ideas ready and know the deals that you've worked on well.

Chapter IV

OUT OF BUSINESS SCHOOL

You're in business school. Maybe you have previous banking, consulting, private equity, or industry experience. Or perhaps you lack finance experience altogether. In any case, you want to know what you can do to increase your chances of getting a hedge fund job when you graduate.

As someone currently in business school, you have a better shot at landing a job at a hedge fund than you did just a few years ago. And that's because over the past few years, hedge funds have stepped up their on-campus recruiting at business schools. The increased recruiting has coincided with the tremendous growth in the hedge fund industry and the heightened need for people to help invest the capital that has been raised. As the hiring needs of hedge funds have increased, they have come to see MBAs as a preselected, identifiable pool of qualified, experienced candidates who are eager to work.

Similar to pre-MBA recruiting, when targeting MBAs, hedge funds seek candidates with skills that match their specific investment style. Since it's rare that new skills are acquired during business school, the hiring firms will typically focus on candidates' work experience at the pre-MBA level. One MBA candidate explained that the hedge funds that recruit on campus tend to be those that value fundamental research, not the pure trading shops. Hedge funds are aware that MBAs typically have broad analytical skills that allow them to analyze an individual company and a specific market as well.

Recently Hired MBA

"When looking at MBAs, hedge funds don't want simply a great college student who had a high GPA, worked at a top investment bank or a leading private equity fund, and then went to one of the best business schools. You'd be surprised how many of those people get dinged. From my experience, hedge funds *worry* about the person who shows up and is a worker bee and says, 'Okay, now what?' Hedge funds don't give you companies to analyze like investment banks do. They want people who have personality and desire and will *seek out* the companies in which to invest."

As pointed out in Case Study 11, not all funds exclusively target those MBAs with investment banking backgrounds. As you research the funds that interest you, it's important to find out the backgrounds of the people who work there. We recommend targeting a fund that has hired people with similar backgrounds to yours. While some funds insist on previous investing or private equity experience, there are others that specifically *don't* want people with that background because they believe it will be harder to get them to conform to their style of investing. Those funds may be open to candidates with more varied backgrounds. There are also funds that are open to people who have experience at long-only asset management firms and others that will bring on sell-side equity researchers. There's no doubt that the network you are building in business school is a valuable asset. A strong network means information, and information can mean investment opportunities, and that is what most hedge funds are ultimately looking for. (See Figure 4.1.)

The director of human resources (HR) at a major fundamental long/short hedge fund explained that funds like his have to look at MBAs because there "simply are not enough i-banking analysts to go around." He points out that there has been a growing interest among hedge funds for MBA talent. "A portfolio manager who has an MBA and went to XYZ business school will be more inclined to hire out of that same school."

The HR director adds that funds know very well the differences between pre-MBA hires and those who have gone through business school. "With a 24-year-old you are getting a candidate who is fundamentally sound, can do research, and may know some companies, but not in depth. With a business school grad you are getting a more

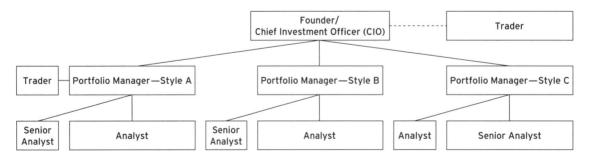

In this model, each portfolio manager would focus on a specific style; for example, event-driven, distressed debt, or long/short.

Figure 4.1 Organizational Chart: Multitier, Multi-strategy P&L Model

experienced, more mature individual. An MBA needs less training and may have a history in a specific sector and some contacts as well." Finally, he notes that the roles are not interchangeable, so a lot of the hiring at the MBA level will come from funds looking for a more polished investment professional.

POSITIONING YOURSELF

As someone coming out of business school, you will have to work with (and overcome) the lack of a hiring cycle. If hedge funds recruit at your school, your interviews may not happen until the spring of your second year when many of your classmates may have already been interviewed for and accepted jobs in other industries (if your school is not targeted by hedge funds, you will have to be more proactive about getting your interviews). Having said that, if you are committed to hedge funds, don't get nervous if you are without a job when January of your second year rolls around.

Our basic advice to MBAs is not too different than what it is for pre-MBAs. To review, that means:

- Read up on hedge funds.
- Understand the different strategies.
- Know yourself—figure out your own strategy and have a seamless story to tell about why you want to work in a hedge fund.
- Know what you bring to the table and why it sets you apart from others.
- Be genuinely interested in investing and be able to express that interest with superb communications skills.
- Make good use of your summers.
- Join your school investment/hedge fund club.

If you are just beginning business school, there are a few things you can do to help improve your chances. We strongly recommend doing what you can to get a summer internship at a hedge fund while in business school. In addition to giving you an introduction to hedge funds, it could pave the way to a permanent position upon graduation. Many firms post internship openings at business schools. If your school doesn't get postings, we recommend using your personal and professional network to land such a position. Your business school professors could also be a source of contacts in the industry.

Glocap Insight	We've seen more and more MBAs who had private equity experience before business school, and therefore would have been destined to join a private equity fund in a career-track position, choosing instead to join a hedge fund after graduation. Of those who make that switch, we estimate about 80% join the hedge fund where they interned for the summer during business school. It's like they're taking a test drive over the summer to see if they enjoy it.

For those who lack finance and/or investing experience, any courses offered by your school on topics such as hedging, appropriate use of leverage, generalist versus sector-specific approaches, accounting, financial analysis, and risk would be useful additions to the standard financial statement analysis courses that you should be taking. There are some schools—Columbia Business School is one that we know of—that offer courses in investing taught by adjunct professors from hedge funds. If yours has similar courses, you would be wise to take advantage of them. (For a typical organizational chart of a multi-tier, multi-strategy P&L model, see Figure 4.1.)

CASE STUDIES

Interestingly, the authors of these case studies all say they would not have gotten into hedge funds had it not been for their business school experience. While they had strong backgrounds, they didn't have the typical banking/finance experience that would have made their paths into hedge funds a bit smoother.

Case Study 9: Getting In with a Banking/Venture Capital Background

This person started out in an investment banking program, moved into venture capital (VC), and then went to business school before landing a hedge fund position.

■ ■ ■

In my case, business school provided me with access to interviews and firms that I wouldn't have had otherwise. I also got to interact with other people interested in hedge funds, and that helped solidify my own interest.

I graduated from college in 2000 with a degree in philosophy/economics. I was uncertain of my career prospects and was thinking of academia or perhaps law school. Fortunately for me, I landed a summer job at a New York-based venture capital fund following my junior year of college. I had no idea what venture capital was and had never seen a balance sheet at the time. I worked with an associate who was fresh out of the business school that I would attend a few years later, and he explained the industry to me. It was hard not to get excited about venture capital in 2000, and the experience opened my eyes to investing. I received an offer to return full-time.

Despite the offer of full-time employment, I felt I should learn about finance. So, I spent October to December of that year applying to investment banking analyst programs and was accepted into the M&A group of a bulge-bracket firm. During my program I learned modeling, basic/advanced finance, and, just as important, a lot of professionalism. Times have changed over the past few years. I'm aware that now some hedge funds approach analysts during the first year of their programs. That wasn't the case when I was in the program, as hedge funds did very little recruiting from the analyst programs. Private equity firms did recruit and I got some offers, but I wanted to go back to VC investing and accepted a position at another New York–based fund.

After two years at the VC fund I applied to business schools. I was stuck and knew that if I wanted to be on partner track in venture capital I would need an MBA. I got into a top business school and spent the summer after my first year at a small private equity fund. I found private equity to be very deal intensive and much more legal work than I like. I had a lot of friends who were in hedge funds and they seemed happy, so I began researching that industry. By the end of the summer I decided to pursue hedge funds. My change was influenced by the inherent differences between hedge funds and private equity. I was interested in the public markets and knew that I preferred the analysis component of my private equity experience to the deal-making component. Hedge funds generally don't do deals—they do more investment analysis. I looked into the various hedge fund styles in the landscape and learned as much as I could. I concluded that long/short equity investing with a value bias spoke most to my prior experience and interests. At such a fund I knew I would be working with companies and doing deep research focusing on cash flows. I missed the first round of on-campus interviews, but was able to get interviews with some of the funds that came to campus in October and November—even though that was a little late in the year to be just beginning.

I found it tough to distinguish myself during on-campus interviews. Everyone looks the same. We all had private equity and/or investment banking experience and wanted to work at a hedge fund. So, I tried to tell my story the best way possible. The funds that come to campus conduct blocks of interviews with 20 people each day so you don't have much time to explain yourself. It's a lot different from when you would interview out of an analyst program. At that stage, it's likely a headhunter has pitched you to a hedge fund so the fund already knows about you before you walk in the door. In business school, all they're going on is a resume. I think my resume was attractive to hedge funds because of my finance/private equity experience, coupled with my clear interest in the public markets (I was a member of the investing club).

"From my experience, some hedge funds don't seem to care what you did in the past. Others want only people with MBAs. What they all want are people who can step in and hit the ground running from day one."

Although I did only a little investing on my own, I don't think that hurt me a great deal. I knew I would be asked for investment ideas during my interviews, so I made sure I had a few that I was comfortable talking about. I was also given the prerequisite technical questions and brainteasers. I recall being given the scenario: You have companies A and B. One has a higher EBITDA and the other has a more levered balance sheet. Which situation would you rather have?

On the personal side I was asked about myself and if I liked working in a collaborative environment. I felt that was an important question because at a hedge fund you spend a lot of time working by yourself and you have to know that going in. If your expectation is that the environment will be like private equity, then you will find it difficult to adjust.

I came out of the process with offers from two very large funds and one small one and went with the small one. All three were research/value-oriented long/short equity funds. From my experience, some hedge funds don't seem to care what you did in the past.

Others want only people with MBAs. What they all want are people who can step in and hit the ground running from day one. In my opinion, the MBA gives you an edge, but it's a longer-term edge. My network is profound. But will people who pick stocks think it matters? No. I think the business school network pays bigger dividends in other industries. I've noticed that few successful hedge fund managers are business school grads.

My advice to anyone looking to get into a hedge fund would be to get intimately familiar with the public markets and learn how to invest. I would definitely suggest doing more investing on your own than I did. The investment banking training is invaluable. Nevertheless, if you can get a good job without going to an investment bank you should consider it. It's all about your risk appetite. Funds can blow up. If you join a hedge fund without prior job experience and it blows up, then where will you be? The current landscape is so uncertain/new that it is hard to tell what would happen to people with hedge fund–only experience in a downturn. It's unclear if the skills are in any way transferable.

Case Study 10: Making Up for No Finance Experience

Having no background in finance and having worked only in start-up technology companies, this person used his international experience and MBA to land a position with a fund that needed someone with precisely his background.

■ ■ ■

I'm convinced I wouldn't have gotten a hedge fund job if I hadn't gone to business school. Not only did I have a background devoid of any finance and investing, but before I went to business school I hardly knew what a hedge fund was. I graduated from an Ivy League school in 1999 with a degree in computer science and followed that with a master's in computer science. At the time I wasn't sure what I wanted to do—maybe get into business or start my own (2000 was still a pretty exciting time for start-ups). I didn't really know what investment banking was except for the long hours and therefore didn't pursue that option.

Although I had offers from small and large technology companies, I ended up joining a seven-person software start-up and spent two years doing a mix of consulting and engineering work. To learn about the business side, I gravitated more to the company's IT (information technology) consulting operations. When this company closed, I had the option of joining one of its client companies (a major media conglomerate) or another technology start-up. I chose the latter and spent two years as director of business development for Asia. While at this company I began to think seriously about business school (the company was founded by a graduate of the MBA program that I eventually attended). I was still unfamiliar with finance, and I thought an MBA would help me become well rounded and maybe get me into venture capital.

I got into a top business school and while there spent a lot of time evaluating my career options. I'd say I was a very confused individual during those two years and debated going into finance or sticking with technology and going to a VC fund. My indecisiveness was helped when I landed a summer research job at a $2 billion long/ short hedge fund. I had interviewed for summer internships with some investment banks, investment management firms, and VC funds. More than anything, I think timing had a lot to do with me landing and accepting an internship at a hedge fund. By the time this hedge fund posted the position on my school's database it was March and a lot of my classmates had already accepted summer positions. I was fortunate that I had not yet accepted an offer from an investment bank.

Honestly, I didn't think I had a background that would fit with a hedge fund. I had never invested on my own and the work at the hedge fund was very new to me. I learned a lot that summer, starting from where to find appropriate information to how to form investment decisions and execute trades (timing, etc.). At the end of the summer, I realized that I liked investing and finance and enjoyed the strategic thinking involved in hedge funds—trying to pick which companies are the winners and which are the losers. At the same time, I also knew I wanted to stay involved with technology, so when I got back to school I decided to pursue hedge funds along with venture capital. Still, those are two different animals with different networks to tap and it was challenging to pursue both avenues.

There were a good number of hedge funds that recruited on campus, but many tended to focus on people who had banking, private equity, or investment experience. My lack of finance hindered my progress with hedge funds. I probably wouldn't have even gotten interviews with hedge funds if it weren't for my summer experience. In addition, initially I wanted to go home to the West Coast and limited my choices to funds in my hometown. Unfortunately, that restriction reduced my options. I did what I could. Hedge funds and VC firms tended to recruit late in the year, so I spent the first semester preparing for interviews and networking. I even flew home on my own dime to meet with firms that I knew weren't interviewing.

When March rolled around, I started to get nervous, as many classmates were either contemplating job offers or had already accepted positions. I knew that the time frame of recruitment for hedge funds and VCs is much later (some classmates received offers from VCs in May and June), but not having an offer in March still bothered me. When a job offer at a hedge fund in my hometown that I had been pur- suing for six months finally fell through, I decided to broaden my search by looking at opportunities in other cities on the West Coast and in the East as well.

I finally got an offer for a VC job at the end of March/beginning of April and was close to landing an offer at another VC firm. Then I got a call from a hedge fund that ironically had gotten my name from another fund at which I had interviewed. The hedge fund was looking for someone who had an international background, especially in Asia, and who knew technology. I think my MBA degree and summer experience, as well as an investment project I did at school, helped round out my credentials.

The interviews focused on my background and new investment ideas. I didn't get grilled too severely compared to some of my other interviews. I was able to present an investment thesis I had done during the previous semester. I had also done a project over the summer and used that as well. During my three rounds of interviews I met everybody on this fund's investment team. I'd say that hedge funds do not care as much about your pedigree as they do about your skill set and ability to form your own investment theses. Maybe that's the reason why many investment professionals at hedge funds do not have a CFA (Chartered Financial Analyst designation), compared to the large numbers that do at brokerage and mutual fund companies. Hedge funds want someone who can come in and hit the ground running. In my case, I spoke English, Korean, and Japanese and I had the industry knowledge and network. My finance background was still not very strong, but this fund traditionally hired people with industry backgrounds and that benefited me.

> *"I'd say that hedge funds do not care as much about your pedigree as they do about your skill set and ability to form your own investment theses."*

For me, business school definitely helped. And the fact that I went to a top school gave me a strong network that I would not have had if I had attended a second- or third-tier school. Of the professionals on my current team, the ones who did go to business school came from an industry background, as I did. The ones with a finance background generally have no MBA. I'd say hedge funds that recruit at business schools look for a level of maturity that they can't find in younger, pre-MBA candidates. And the networks help as well.

I can comfortably say that, as to operations, hedge funds run very similarly to any business start-ups. The management does not have time to baby employees but rather wants to hire entrepreneurial and ambitious/proactive personalities who can learn on their own and contribute in whatever ways they can. In that sense, when you are meeting with recruiters, you should present yourself as a capable investor with experience instead of a young person with potential but in need of guidance/development. Additionally, networking is important. Portfolio managers do not have time to go through resumes and interview many candidates. Recommendations from colleagues/ friends can make their lives much easier. Knowing people in the industry is invaluable.

Case Study 11: Benefiting from Solid Summers

This is another MBA who had no previous banking or finance experience. To combat that, he made good use of his summers while in graduate school and showed extra determination to beat out his classmates who had the backgrounds typically sought by hedge funds.

■ ■ ■

Although my background was anything but typical, I believe I got a position at a leading hedge fund because of my determination and persistence. I graduated from an Ivy League school with a liberal arts degree. Instead of going off to investment banks and consulting firms as many classmates did, I wanted to do something different and decided to spend two years living and working abroad. At the time I thought I could always go to business school later if I wanted to do something more mainstream.

After returning from living abroad, I applied to several joint degree programs because I wanted a broad education. Since I didn't have much business experience, I got a lot out of the MBA degree. Every class, no matter what the subject, enabled me to learn about a company's business model and how to assess it. In particular, strategy, corporate finance, and accounting classes were extremely helpful. If you are breaking into investing for the first time, it is imperative to make great use of your summers. Because I was in a joint degree program, I had more than one summer to gain experience. I spent one summer in the M&A group of a bulge-bracket investment bank, and the other in the hedge fund arm of the same bank. One of the differences that I found between hedge fund recruiting and investment banking recruiting is that hedge funds typically won't make an offer unless they know it will be accepted. Whereas some major banks may bring on 60 to 80 MBAs, a leading hedge fund may bring on only one or two, so they are not in the practice of extending more offers than the number of available slots. This translates into it typically taking more time and a greater showing of commitment to secure an offer from a hedge fund. As well, hedge funds seem to rarely parallel process candidates. This means that, while they may initially interview 15 candidates on campus, they may take only one or two candidates through the entire process at a time. If they don't make an offer (or have it accepted), the fund may then circle back to the initial pool of 15. The single processing means that sometimes it takes weeks for the fund to get back to someone after the first interview.

I quickly learned that taking a targeted approach to interviews is the best strategy when seeking a hedge fund job. Although I had learned a fair amount of financial modeling through my summer jobs, I still didn't have the finance experience that many of my classmates did. While I followed companies throughout business school, I didn't do any investing on my own. I did have a mock portfolio, but my impression was that funds would rather have seen me investing my own money and feeling the anxiety of having money at risk, even if it was just a few hundred dollars.

At my business school the hedge funds weren't usually part of the first wave of recruiting that occurred from September to December. In fact, many friends who were going for hedge fund jobs were still looking in May of their final year. It was hard to get around the fact that most funds wanted people with two years of banking and two years of private equity experience. These are the people who tend to have the best analytical experience and may also have had exposure to the public markets. In that environment I was a rarity. It took a lot of legwork to get in the door, but I found that due to my summer experience, funds were always willing to meet me. If I had not had summer experience in investing, I am really not sure what I would have done.

For the funds that came to campus I was able to drop my resume and get an interview. For most on-campus interviews the funds usually met with me and 30 others with the desired background. I had high grades and test scores and had worked at leading firms, but my experience was slight compared to the banking and private equity guys.

Rather than defend my career choices or look silly trying to play down the great experience my classmates had, I tried to play up my passion for event-driven investing and how my joint degree made me a great fit. I ran a completely targeted search focusing only on funds that did event-driven investing. I made a point of emphasizing what I wanted to do and explaining why, and that resonated with the places where I interviewed.

At the fund where I eventually accepted a job, the first round of interviews was on campus. I was first asked a series of personality/fit questions—What's your background? Why are you interested in investing? What style are you interested in? In nearly all of my interviews it was pointed out to me that I didn't have an investing background. Once I was told that, I would typically steer the interview toward my strength by saying something like, "Let me show you my ideas. I think you'll be impressed by how much I know, given my background." Following the personality/fit questions, I was grilled to see my thought process. I was peppered with questions such as: What do you think about XX industry in general?

The next meeting was at the fund's headquarters and was again split between fit and investing-specific questions. The fit ones were: Why do you want to do event-driven investing? Why did you go to business school? Then I was asked: What industries do you like? What do you think makes a company a good company or a bad one? What companies do you like? As well, I was always asked to present an investment idea I was currently most excited about. In addition to these interviews with investment professionals, I also met with the operations professionals, such as the head accountant and general counsel. It was important to the firm that I be a good fit with the entire team.

> *"The last thing a hedge fund wants is someone with a great resume who is just waiting for things to come to them."*

The third meeting was a three-part interview. Some funds can be tough and try to rattle you. This one was not like that. The first portion of the interview was to see how I look at companies. In addition to asking me point-blank questions they also presented me with some scenarios: "Say you have two manufacturing companies. One is big and one is small. In a market downturn, what would you want to find out to determine which would fare better?" For the second part I was given the financial statements of a company and asked to calculate 20 different values such as market value, enterprise value, EBITDA, and free cash flow. Last was a case study. I was given the financials of a company and two hours to come up with a presentation for the partners.

My overall advice to someone in business school who has banking experience would be to target your search and spend time thinking about the style of investing that interests you and be able to explain why it does. And, above all, you have to demonstrate that you are aggressive and hungry. The last thing a hedge fund wants is someone with a great resume who is just waiting for things to come to them. At a hedge fund, deals won't be coming in the door waiting for you to execute them. If you have the right background a fund will have no doubt that you can build a financial model and do the finance-related work. What they really want to know is if you think differently than the hundreds of other people who have a similar background. Will you bring new ideas?

Chapter V

GETTING IN LATER IN YOUR CAREER

In addition to the increased need for junior staff, we've seen a greater number of hedge funds seeking investment professionals who can step in and hit the ground running, and this has created opportunities for more seasoned people.

Given the absence of an identifiable pool of more senior talent, hedge funds have sought more experienced talent from other hedge funds, private equity funds, investment banks, long-only asset management firms, and various other sell-side positions. As you read the case studies in this chapter, you will see that the requirements to get into a hedge fund later in your career are not that different from those mentioned earlier in this book. Hiring firms still want to see that you have a passion for investing. They will expect that you can flawlessly analyze and value a company and can dissect all financial statements. And, just as with the more junior roles, they will want to see that your skills mesh with their investment style; for example, someone from a long-only asset management fund would most likely not be a fit at a credit fund, nor, most likely, would a sell-side equity researcher be a fit at a quant shop. The more senior hires will be expected to have investment ideas and be able to present those ideas with impeccable communication skills.

Whether you join from an investment bank, a private equity fund, an asset management firm, or sell-side equity research, as someone who is more senior you will be expected to bring very tangible experience to the table and be able to hit the ground running. You may also be expected to show visible proof of your track record. For people coming from the buy side this can be the performance of your funds, while for researchers it could be a specific long or short recommendation you made (this should outline when you made the call, where the price was, and what happened). As someone who has been out of school and may be well into your professional career, we recommend using your personal and professional network to help advance your job search.

INDUSTRY EXPERTISE

As hedge funds have grown into large, institutional managers, many have adopted structures that feature investment professionals with industry specializations (for example, healthcare or technology) and this represents an opportunity for people with these skills. One pool of candidates is sell-side equity researchers. These individuals already follow a specific sector and can continue their coverage while making a move to the buy side. The need for industry expertise has also created an opening for people with less traditional backgrounds. For example, someone who worked at a notable technology company and has an MBA from a top school can combine that expertise to seek a position as a telecom/tech analyst. Similarly, someone who was premed or even a practicing physician could be attractive to a long/short fund looking for a healthcare analyst, provided that person has some type of business/consulting experience and has an interest in the public markets. If you have specific industry experience we suggest approaching hedge funds directly and pitching yourself as someone who can step in and help research and choose the right investments in your field.

LATERAL MOVES

One of the most obvious places to find a seasoned hedge fund professional is another hedge fund. Lateral moves are more common in hedge funds than they are in other industries (in particular private equity) because your long-term equity is not tied up. Your performance will be evaluated each year, and this is especially true for people who get a percentage of profits. If you are at a firm where you are paid on your own profit and loss (P&L), then it will be easy for the next firm to judge you—it's simply how you are paid. Junior positions don't have separate P&L, so it is important to record your own performance in case you want to show it to someone. We recommend keeping as detailed a record as possible with the date you made a specific recommendation, the price fluctuations of the stock (or other security you recommended), and the effect on the fund. You should also show directly or indirectly how you were paid on your call and why you recommended the investment/sale. This should be a detailed spreadsheet with reasons attached so you can defend your performance. Table 5.1 is an example of such a spreadsheet. Note: The candidate whose picks are reflected in the table was an analyst at a long/short equity fund (the grayed sections were recommendations that did not make it into the portfolio).

Table 5.1   Candidate 1–Self-Generated Investment Ideas

Stock	Investment Type	Put in Portfolio	Avg. Rec. Price	Div. Yield	Current Price	Unrealized % Gain	Avg. Exit Price	Realized % Gain
Company A	Long	Yes	$46.00		$73.50	59.8%	$61.00	33%
Company B	Long	Yes	$11.50		$28.00	143.5%	$17.50	52%
Company C	Long	Yes	$20.85	12%	$24.00	27.1%		
Company D	Long	Yes	$32.25		$43.35	34.4%		
Company E	Long	Yes	$8.50		$11.50	35.3%	$11.50	35%
Company F	Long	Yes	$13.86		$18.20	31.3%		
Company G	Long	Yes	$11.75		$16.40	39.6%	$13.75	17%
Company H	Long	Yes	$14.00		$20.32	45.1%	$17.00	21%
Company I	Long	Yes	$17.50		$16.89	−3.5%	$16.50	−6%
Company J	Long	Yes	$19.50		$21.50	10.3%	$16.50	−15%
Company K	Long	Yes	$12.00		$13.23	10.3%		
Company L	Long	No	$56.00		$65.32	16.6%		
Company M	Long	No	$11.00	16%	$12.92	33.5%		
Company N	Long	No	$9.60		$14.00	45.8%		
Company O	Long	No	$24.00		$34.80	45.0%		
Company P	Long	No	$8.25		$16.75	103.0%		
Company Q	Long	No	$21.50		$27.44	27.6%		
Company R	Long	No	$23.50		$32.59	38.7%		
Company S	Long	No	$20.50		$28.00	36.6%		
Company T	Short	Yes	$15.75		$6.10	61.3%	$10.50	33.3%
Company U	Short	Yes	$12.00		$5.05	57.9%	$9.00	25.0%
Company V	Short	Yes	$8.50		$5.39	36.6%	$6.00	29.4%
Company W	Short	Yes	$5.25		$2.30	56.2%	$4.00	23.8%
Company X	Short	Yes	$11.41		$14.50	−27.1%		
Company Y	Short	Yes	$7.00		$5.70	18.6%	$5.25	25.0%
Company Z	Short	Yes	$45.00		$41.00	8.9%	$41.50	7.8%
Company AA	Short	Yes	$19.50		$22.45	−15.1%		
Company BB	Short	Yes	$40.00		$47.00	−17.5%		
Company CC	Short	Yes	$17.50			100.0%	$15.00	14.3%
Company DD	Short	Yes	$20.50		$7.35	64.1%	$17.00	17.1%

(Continued)

Table 5.1   (Continued)

Returns Analysis–Assuming Equal Weighting		Hit Rate Analysis	Up	Down	% Hits
Unrealized Total Picks	37.2%	All Ideas–Realized/Unrealized	25	6	80.6%
Unrealized Total Longs	40.5%	All Longs–Realized/Unrealized	17	2	89.5%
Unrealized Total Shorts	31.3%	All Shorts–Realized/Unrealized	8	4	66.7%

Total Portfolio Returns–Candidate 1 Picks[a]

Portfolio Position Longs	22.6%
Portfolio Position Shorts	16.8%
Total Portfolio Positions	19.7%

Total Picks Candidate 1–Realized + Unrealized[b]

Longs	30.9%
Shorts	16.8%
Total	25.6%

Total Picks–Not Included in Portfolio	43.4%

Source: Glocap Search LLC.

[a]Includes only self-generated ideas that were included in the portfolio (included positions at exit prices).
[b]Includes positions not included in the portfolio. For ones in the portfolio, included positions at exit prices.

INTERVIEWS

Given a candidate's work experience, interviews at this stage tend to be more heavily focused on fit. Hiring firms will also want to see that your investment style is compatible with their own. One individual who made the switch described his interviews:

> I found that once you have already worked at a hedge fund, interviewing for a lateral move is a less painful process. At this point it was fairly well understood that I could do the job, so the interviews focused more on personality and how smart they thought I was. I knew I would be asked for investment write-ups, so I always had three ready to give out.

The interviews at this level can also be pretty quick—and that mirrors how things will be at the hedge fund, where the predominant requirement can be to work fast and be thorough. The same person goes on to say:

> At this fund I talked with the other analysts. There was some small talk about current events, but they got right to the point pretty quickly. In addition to the investment write-ups, they asked what type of information sources I used (Bloomberg, etc.). Did I have a network of bankers to call on deals in the market? I was asked about past investments such as: What did you make money on? What did you lose money on? And, of course: Why did you leave your previous fund? There were no trick questions, brainteasers, psychological tests, or handwriting analyses. At this point they really want to know your investment ideas.

CASE STUDIES

To follow are case studies of five people who broke into hedge funds later in their careers. Of the five examples, one joined from private equity, the second moved over from a family office, another switched from sell-side equity research, a fourth broke in after working in an investment bank, and the last transitioned in after working at a long-only asset management firm.

Case Study 12: From Private Equity into Hedge Funds

This person spent a couple of years at a private equity shop before making the transition into a hedge fund. This is a good example of someone who got into a fund a little later in their career.

■ ■ ■

Before hedge funds my entire career had been in private equity. Looking back, I think my background and being able to apply private equity style due diligence to public company investing helped me make it into hedge funds. My father had been active in private equity, so I was familiar with it from an early age. By the time I got to college—class of 1999 from an Ivy League school with a degree in finance and accounting—I knew I wanted to pursue private equity. I had done a seven-month internship in the acquisitions department of a major hotel chain during my junior year, and that experience gave me the basic skill set (financial modeling, etc.) to bypass the banking program that most undergrads have to go through. Instead, I was hired directly into the merchant banking group of a major Wall Street firm. My goal had been to eventually own and operate my own company and, outside of just doing it outright, I thought there was no better way to learn how to acquire and operate a business than by working at a private equity fund.

I worked at the merchant bank for three years, during which time I sourced deals; performed financial analysis, industry analysis, and due diligence; and monitored portfolio companies. I worked on management buyouts, follow-on deals, mergers, and refinancings. In all, I participated in the acquisitions of seven companies. I had a chance to join a private equity fund that specialized in turnaround opportunities. This was

2003 and the turnaround space was a niche practice and a hot place to be. I worked on all aspects of identifying, investing in, turning around, and restructuring several companies. After two years at this fund I got a random call from a headhunter seeking to fill a position at a hedge fund. I wasn't thinking hedge funds at the time, so they had to sell me on the opportunity to bring my private equity experience and apply it to the public markets. The timing was right as well. My firm wanted me to go on to get my MBA, but I had no interest in going back to school. The new firm was a multi-strategy shop that had a carve-out dedicated to the public markets.

Despite my strong background in principal investing, mergers and acquisitions, finance, and accounting, I was still subjected to a grueling interview process. The first-round interview was an informal hour-long interview. That was followed by a series of interviews over the course of a few weeks with about a half dozen junior people at the firm. Their questions were also mostly personality/fit ones, though they all wanted to know why I had left the merchant bank and why I was looking to leave my current job. Then I was given a 10-hour, on-site case study. I was told to analyze a pending merger between two companies and to figure out the proper valuation of each company's stock, and if I would go long or short. For this exercise it was me and one of the firm's partners in a room mapping out the merger on a whiteboard. It was completely interactive and unlike other case studies I had done. This was a very intellectual shop, and there was definitely a correct answer, which had to be figured out mathematically. It was an absolutely binary process, as they hired all three people who got to the right answer. I later learned the case study was given to about 150 people and that the firm had wanted to hire four or five people but couldn't find any others to pass the test. Once I had passed the case study, I met the firm's three partners (there was no reason for them to waste time meeting anyone who didn't pass the test). They mostly asked about my background, growing up, my family, and what I liked to do with my free time. At this point, I knew I was on my way to getting an offer.

"Fit is definitely a two-way street, and job candidates should think long and hard about the people they will be working with."

In hindsight, I wish I had done more of my own due diligence. This firm spent many hours and had several people meet with me to learn about my personality and to determine whether they thought I would fit in with them. I should have done the same. Fit is definitely a two-way street, and job candidates should think long and hard about the people they will be working with. You have to be just as comfortable working with them as they are with you.

I'd recommend speaking with junior people at the firm to get an idea of what working at the fund is like. I've found that there is a bond between junior people across firms—we know each other socially and are often from the same schools—and therefore we are usually willing to help each other out. The person with whom I ended up working was very different from how he appeared when I met him during interviews, and after a year I knew it wasn't the right place for me. I had pitched three investment ideas and they didn't act on any of them. By sourcing my own ideas I felt I was doing just what they wanted me to, but I was stymied by a personality clash. Finally, after one of my rejected ideas tripled in price

I started looking at other opportunities. The people at the firm agreed that the situation wasn't working.

In my search for a new position I used headhunters and my own contacts—friends, fraternity brothers, former colleagues, and so on. I've found that headhunters are firmly entrenched in the industry and certainly made my life easier.

Once you are being interviewed at the VP level, hiring firms focus more on your track record. I had five interviews and got four offers. I was still subjected to case studies and personality tests and was asked for investment ideas, of which I had plenty. At one firm I was given the name of a company and asked to come back in a week with my investment opinion. I built my models, wrote an investment memo, and made the appropriate industry calls. At the end of the day I felt the company was overvalued and would not make a good investment. I came out with a short recommendation. The firm at which I was interviewing agreed with me, and its own valuation was not much different from the one I came up with. This proved to me that being intellectually honest with oneself is paramount, and this is a piece of advice I give to others. In case studies it may be tempting to search for and come up with a buy recommendation. But, if you do your analysis and come to the conclusion that something is not a good investment, then don't be timid about saying so. Be true to your convictions and what has worked for you in the past.

A similar thing happened when I pitched an idea during interviews at my current firm. Although they said it wasn't their type of deal, they heard me out and saw my thought process and must have liked my way of thinking because here I am. We are a turnaround PE shop that has recently raised a securities fund. This fund is long only and applies a PE mentality to the public markets, where we hold positions for three to five years. I've been here six months and have pitched six ideas, and the firm has put money to work in four of them.

I would advise anyone who says they want to get into a hedge fund to think long and hard about what they want. If you want to be a public markets investor, then go to a hedge fund. If you want to run your own company, then private equity would be a better choice.

In my case, I'm very happy that I did five years of private equity before joining a hedge fund. In my experience, it's easy to switch from private equity to a hedge fund, but not the other way around.

I wholeheartedly recommend going into a two-year analyst program where one would get broad finance experience, learn modeling, and work on a high volume of transactions. Within investment banking I'd suggest getting into leveraged finance, M&A, or equity capital markets. I would advise *against* going into a hedge fund directly out of college. I just can't see someone being ready to make a meaningful contribution at that point in their career. In addition, it's a less structured work environment without a formal training program.

I would add that the unsystematic nature of the hedge fund recruiting process makes it more stressful than searching for a position in private equity. Since hedge funds are not out there recruiting at the same time, there is a lack of structure that can create huge time gaps between interviews. I'd say the timing issue makes balancing the hedge fund recruiting process quite difficult and is something new candidates should know about. You could receive exploding offers while still going down the road with other shops.

In terms of interviewing, I'd say you should practice enough so your answers become second nature. Don't BS your interviewers. Make sure you can speak to everything on your resume, and don't list deals that you can't speak about for at least 30 minutes. You don't want to look like an idiot. You should be able to spin any experience that you've had into something that would apply to the job you're interviewing for.

See Resume F in Appendix B on page 168.

Case Study 13: A Family Office Becomes a Stepping-Stone

This person didn't focus on a career in hedge funds early on. After completing a banking program he had two different jobs—one at a firm doing acquisitions and another at a family office doing public investing.

■ ■ ■

I was an economics major at a small liberal arts college and had no visions of hedge funds. Even though I didn't have a finance background I interviewed at some investment banks and consulting firms and ended up getting into an investment banking analyst program. I worked in the leveraged finance group and stayed there for three years (the bulk of my colleagues began looking for opportunities after about 18 months—mostly in private equity because at the time hedge funds were not as popular). I knew I wanted to explore opportunities outside of banking, and I looked around a little but didn't get excited about much that was out there. I finally joined a venture-funded education company in Boston doing business and corporate development with an emphasis on acquisitions. I ended up working there for about two years and left soon after the firm was bought by a major media company.

Fortunately, I had stayed in contact with former colleagues from my banking program and through someone I met there was able to join the private equity group of an investment firm that managed the capital of a high net worth individual. During my time there (almost six years), I was able to work on some public market investments, which I found I enjoyed more than private equity. This firm was value focused and maintained a long-term bias with a three- to six-year time horizon.

I wasn't necessarily looking to join a hedge fund. The opportunity to work at my current firm really came through some contacts I had kept in touch with. They knew that I had spent time working on both public and private investments and therefore had a unique investing skill set. They recommended me for my current position. However, I still had to go through a lengthy interview process (it lasted several months). My first meeting was a friendly get-to-know-you session. After that, I was asked to analyze two specific companies and develop an investment opinion for both. It was a very busy time at my current job, so I took a couple of weeks to complete my work. This was an intense exercise, but I had relevant experience, having worked in an investing capacity for more than five years. This was a great opportunity for the team to get a sense of how I thought about investing and vice versa. I prepared a comprehensive analysis and presentation outlining my views and recommendations. My approach was to act as if I were working at the firm and presenting views either to my fellow investment professionals or to the management team of a company in which we were considering investing. Since I knew that fit goes both ways, in addition to trying to make the people with whom I was meeting comfortable with me, I also wanted to make sure that I would like working with them. Therefore, when I presented to the team, I made sure that I had questions for them; we had a very good, thoughtful conversation as a result. That's when I knew the fit made sense.

After presenting to the investment team, I received good feedback from the recruiter. The next step was a dinner with a few members of the investment team. I saw this as their opportunity to engage me on a personal level. Like many hedge funds, this one is small and we all sit on the trading floor in close proximity; personal chemistry is very important. After some more positive feedback, the fund spent about three weeks placing reference calls. I finally received a verbal offer at a dinner with the head of the firm, nearly four months after my initial meeting.

I wasn't a stereotypical investor who began reading the *Wall Street Journal* at a young age and buying stocks for my own account. In my case, I benefited from my investment banking experience, which gave me a solid foundation in corporate finance, and also from my private equity investing experience at the family office where I worked.

> "I would recommend that those interested in hedge funds figure out what they like and don't like."

My advice to others who aspire to work in a hedge fund would be to get the investment banking training under your belt. I don't think the particular group matters, as most will give you a solid foundation in finance, capital structures, M&A, and financings. I would recommend that those interested in hedge funds figure out what they like and don't like. In my case, I didn't like the deal environment of private equity. It made me feel more like a lawyer than an investor; I wanted to spend 100% of my time thinking about businesses and investing rather than negotiating purchase agreements. It's a very different skill set.

When I interview candidates interested in joining our firm I definitely look for a certain temperament. Our type of investing requires a lot of patience and we target curious, well-rounded, and thoughtful people who are levelheaded and have a lot of conviction when making decisions.

Case Study 14: An Equity Researcher Breaks the Mold

Here's someone who switched into a hedge fund from sell-side equity research. He has a less traditional background, having spent time as a journalist and a United Nations worker.

■■■

I didn't get into a hedge fund until later in my professional career, and my background was a little less traditional. I came out of college with a degree in history in 1987, worked as a journalist for a few years, then got a master's in international relations from a well-known non-U.S. university, and even worked for the United Nations for four years.

After deciding to pursue a career on Wall Street I knew I had to go to business school. I had no experience and no educational background that would lead me into a finance job and most firms wouldn't talk to me until I had an MBA. Since I finished in four straight semesters, I had no summer break with which to pursue an internship. Instead, I worked part-time during school on the emerging markets fixed-income desk of a boutique investment bank doing ad hoc research projects.

I was looking to continue with emerging markets out of school, and my first job was with a hedge fund. I wasn't really focusing on hedge funds, and getting the job was kind of random. I saw something on the career board of my school posted by an alum who was the head of this fund. I ended up leaving after one year when the fund decided to get out of emerging markets after the Russian default/crisis. Admittedly, I was a bit naive about the allure of the compensation structure of hedge funds, or I might have stayed longer or looked to move to another hedge fund. I ended up taking a research role with the emerging markets group of a long-only asset management firm, where I stayed for a little over three years before being laid off.

My next position was as an analyst/portfolio manager with a major pension fund manager. I had been there for four years when another opportunity with a hedge fund came up. The interview process was very informal and lasted about four months, during which time I met with the fund principals twice and every employee of the firm once.

"Contrary to what some hedge funds may think, long-only investing is not a slow and lazy process. There is a lot of trading that goes on."

While it is true that most hedge funds will insist that candidates come in with specific investment ideas that can be backed up with detailed analysis, this didn't happen to me. I was asked what I liked, but most of what I had to do was dispel some of the misconceptions about people making the switch from equity research/long-only portfolio management. Contrary to what some hedge funds may think, long-only investing is not a slow and lazy process. There is a lot of trading that goes on. It also helps to be able to spin your skills in the right way. While long-only managers may not specifically short stocks, the process of being benchmarked against an index requires taking de facto short decisions. For example, if I am looking at four banks in South Africa and like one, I am in essence shorting the other three by not being invested in them. When I explained that concept to hedge funds they got the point.

My advice to people looking to get into hedge funds for the first time, or even for those seeking a lateral move, would be to do your due diligence on the partners and do it quickly. Ask around as much as possible about those you will be working with and for. If you speak with five people in the industry and they all tell you that the people have questionable reputations, then you should probably avoid that fund. I wouldn't limit my research to sell-side people, as many of them may be wary of talking about a client. I'd also recommend you get as much in writing as possible. Finally, be aware of personality issues. Even though it's hard to know what people are like until you are there, whatever idea you can get as to what people will be like will help you in the long run.

Case Study 15: A Banker Gets In

This person has a typical pre-MBA banking background. He spent some time in banking after business school as well, but he knew he wanted to get into a hedge fund. He invested on his own and was very aggressive about the process.

■ ■ ■

I finished undergraduate school in 1996 with a finance degree and was definitely not thinking about hedge funds at the time. In fact, I didn't get into a hedge fund until nine years later. Even though I studied finance I didn't really think too much about where it would lead me, so I felt pretty fortunate that I landed a permanent job doing equity research at an asset management arm of a major Wall Street firm. I was mostly doing quant research and helped this firm put together several equity investment products, and I was hoping to move into a portfolio management role.

I had been there about 18 months and wasn't really looking to make a switch, but a friend who worked at another firm that ran a fund of hedge funds got me an interview. This firm wanted someone to do quant analysis, kind of the grunt work. I went through about three rounds of interviews and spoke with everyone there. There were no tests, but I was definitely grilled pretty hard and was asked a lot of math, quantitative, and valuation questions. I was offered a job at the end of my third interview and I accepted. Even though I was doing pretty well after being hired, I realized that I was not building the right set of skills at the fund to eventually be able to pick stocks. At a minimum, I lacked the most basic skills needed to succeed in investing: valuing companies. That's when I decided to go into banking.

After making the switch into banking I also applied to business school with the thinking that an MBA would open more options for me in the long term. I ended up going to a top five business school and then reentered the workforce in 2002, but that was a tough year to find a job, and I was only getting calls from investment banks. It was a difficult decision, but I ultimately decided to return to banking (and park myself for a few years). Three years into the job, I grew disillusioned and still clung to my goal of picking stocks.

I began thinking seriously about hedge funds in the summer of 2005 and contacted a recruiter later in the year. To me, hedge funds were everything that I had always wanted—they were fast-paced and results-oriented and everybody was held accountable for what they did. I liked that type of culture. My interview process went pretty fast— from the first interview to having an offer in hand was about four weeks. The first round was to see if they would like me. In the second I was grilled on my market knowledge, logic, and valuation skills. As is typical with most hedge funds, I was asked to present a case study on a long or short idea. I had done a lot of investing in college, mainly in high-tech stocks (in fact, at one point I was up $500,000 before losing $150,000). I was pretty much a market junkie and was glued to the markets and my Bloomberg terminal whenever I could be. Even though I didn't do much investing at business school, I think this hedge fund, which is primarily an equities shop, liked the fact that I had not only invested in the markets on my own earlier, but that I had lost a lot of money. It showed them that I could go through a painful experience and that I had learned a lot. I think my varied background in equity research and M&A also helped.

> *"I'd strongly advise people to be opinionated, in fact very opinionated. There is no right or wrong, but you had better have a view and not be wishy-washy."*

In my case I think the fund was looking to bring in someone with a little more seasoning. I've noticed that a lot of hedge funds want to hire mature people who can sit down with a CEO/CFO and ask questions and get answers. A big part of the job is being able to make and maintain relationships with company management. Analysts also need to have enough experience to extract a piece of information without having to ask directly. I believe the skills I picked up in banking set me apart from other candidates. This fund definitely appreciated the fact that I could value a company (and do that valuation from different angles); dissect a financial statement (and understand how the company works, makes money, and grows); and present my views in a clear and concise way (keep it simple and direct).

Now that I'm at a hedge fund it's proving to be everything that I had wanted and then some, and a lot of that is because of the great people here. If I were to advise someone on getting into a hedge fund, I'd say having a strong network is really important. I used a recruiter, but you should not rely on one as your only strategy. I would also recommend that you follow the markets and know the current themes. Lastly (and this is not in order of importance), I'd strongly advise people to be opinionated, in fact very opinionated. There is no right or wrong, but you had better have a view and not be wishy-washy.

See Resume G in Appendix B on page 169.

Case Study 16: From Asset Management to Long/Short Equity

This candidate took a longer route into her hedge fund position. She went into a banking program a few years out of college, worked overseas, and went to business school. She has strong buy-side experience (both during and after business school) and knowledge of Asia, which ultimately made her a fit at a long/short equity fund.

■ ■ ■

I graduated from college in 1996 with a degree in chemical engineering and stayed for another year to get my master's. At the time most of my classmates were going on to medical school or getting their PhDs. Some went into banking and consulting, but I wasn't even thinking of finance and certainly not hedge funds. Were there even hedge funds back then? I took a job as a process engineer at a major pharmaceutical company, making me one of only a handful of chemical engineering majors who actually practiced engineering.

After a little more than a year and a half I realized there was not much creativity to what I was doing and became intrigued with finance. I thought finance would give me exposure to many things that were happening in the business world. And, of course, the lucrative packages did not hurt. I took a little step back by applying and getting into an investment banking analyst program at a bulge-bracket bank. Most of the other analysts were straight out of college, so at the tender age of 25 I felt old, but it didn't matter. I was specifically recruited by the structured products group of this bank, as they had a tough time filling an opening. This was 1999 and the hot thing to do would have been telecom, media, and technology. My background didn't include finance and accounting, but this bank thought engineers, who typically know math, can program, and think logically, would fit well in structured products.

Although I did well in my program, it was a tough 18 months (I had begun in November instead of the usual July). In addition to working very late hours, I studied and got my CFA (Chartered Financial Analyst designation). Toward the end of my program I was sent to Hong Kong to work in the bank's technology banking group. I was able to work on deals with companies in Korea and Taiwan. Unfortunately, the downturn caused by 9/11 led my bank to lay off about 80% of the third-year analyst class. That sudden event expedited my decision to go to business school, and I got into an Ivy League program.

I looked at business school as a way to recraft my life. Since I had gotten my CFA I was interested in investment management—but not hedge funds. My school had a good investment management club, and we spent time pitching investment ideas to senior members of the club and putting actual dollars to work. During the summer I worked in the London offices of a major U.S.-based investment management firm covering Asian consumer stocks. While I had an offer to return to this firm after graduation and work out of its Hong Kong office, I wasn't ready to go back. This was 2004 and there was very little hiring going on. There were some hedge funds that interviewed on campus and I talked with two or three of them, but I wouldn't say my school was a big feeder for hedge funds. There were a lot of active investors, but they all seemed to be Warren Buffett disciples—not the fast-moving hedge fund types. At the end of the day I didn't think a hedge fund would suit me. I knew that research analysts at hedge funds cover many companies and have to come up with quick decisions. I wanted to be afforded the time to develop my research and to become an expert in a smaller group of companies. I also thought it would be easier to make the switch from a mutual fund firm to a hedge fund than vice versa.

Fortunately, I landed a position in the New York office of another U.S.-based asset management firm. I was covering Japanese tech companies. This was exactly what I wanted to be doing—covering Asian stocks from New York.

After about 18 months I felt my role was too limiting and began to look at hedge funds. I didn't have the flexibility to look at other sectors, and the companies in my sector weren't doing much. My firm did have a hedge fund and I could contribute ideas, but it wasn't my primary responsibility. The timing just felt right to move to a hedge fund. I felt I was ready to make the speedy investment decisions expected by a hedge fund and to contribute from day one. On top of that, I knew how the industry worked, how to work with brokers, and how to conduct company meetings.

I worked with a recruiter who sent me on a few interviews. The interviews at the fund that I eventually joined (a long/short equity shop) were a lot more accelerated than others I had gone on. As is the norm, I met everyone at the firm during the course of the interviews. The first round was more of a get-to-know-you/personality one to make sure you're not a psycho. There were no psychological tests. It's the second round where they drill deeper into your investment knowledge and where you have to show you have the passion for investing. If you have that passion, it will come through loud and clear. From my experience, people who make investment decisions have a sixth sense that allows them to size someone up pretty quickly.

I had been investing on my own since business school (though for compliance reasons it was hard to do much while at my most recent job), so I was ready for the investment questions. This fund asked all the standard questions that I had practiced and specifically wanted to know what investment mistakes I had made and what I had learned. They also asked how I differentiate my research and what gives me an edge over others. As was the case with other hedge fund interviews, I was presented with an investment case. For this one, I was given two weeks to research a consumer company and told to come back with an investment decision. This was something I had been doing a lot of, so getting the financials, building a model, and even speaking with company officials were not new for me.

Even though the interviewing was intense, I was surprised at how practical the decision-making process at hedge funds was. At a mutual fund firm there are a lot of procedures to follow for anything you do, be it hiring someone or making a new investment. I found the culture much more fluid at a hedge fund and that was reflected in the interview process. From start to finish my interviews lasted about two weeks. Now, I'm covering Asian stocks.

"I've found that many say they want a hedge fund without knowing why, or maybe they're just thinking about the money. Those types of people will not make it."

Personally, I don't think I would have been ready to work in a hedge fund if I hadn't gone to business school. I had done some investing on my own, but business school and my job after graduation helped me develop and refine my thought processes and decision-making capabilities. Without that I wouldn't have been comfortable applying to a hedge fund.

I believe the value of an MBA in terms of working at a hedge fund is more long-term. The extra experience gives you new perspectives, and meeting people with different investment philosophies exposes you to different modes of thought that you can incorporate into your own thinking. While a 24-year-old can definitely be a good hedge fund analyst (they are certainly more energetic and don't need as much sleep as older people do), a lot of investing is not strictly about modeling. My firm will look to investment banking analysts for junior roles, but for more senior investment positions will seek people with more experience.

Now, many seniors at my alma mater contact me for advice about getting into a hedge fund. The first thing I do is ask why they want to work at a hedge fund. I've found that many say they want a hedge fund without knowing why, or maybe they're just thinking about the money. Those types of people will not make it. Since a lot of the interview process is designed to gauge a candidate's motivation, if someone can't convince me why they want hedge funds there's no way they will be able to convince their interviewers. For those who are absolutely set on hedge funds, I advise them to do as much due diligence about the shops at which they interview as they themselves are subjected to. It's important that you enjoy people you may be working with. Some places can be sweatshops, and that is okay as long as you know what you're getting yourself into. I've heard of one that wants to see performance in your first three months and if you don't deliver you may be out the door.

Chapter VI

FUND MARKETING

Many people probably imagine working at a hedge fund as an analyst or a trader. However, there are other roles that are integral parts of a fund's operations and its eventual success. A few of those positions fall under the general category of fund marketing. This chapter goes over the various fund marketing roles and presents case studies of people who secured those positions. It focuses mostly on junior-level positions, meaning those people looking to break into a fund marketing role at a hedge fund for the first time (the more senior-level investor relations and fund-raising positions are usually filled by people moving laterally from other hedge funds or other types of asset management firms). To stress what hedge funds look for when hiring various types of marketers, we thought it would be helpful to show some actual job specifications from recent searches on which we worked (you will find these toward the middle of the chapter).

From our experience, there will always be a need for marketers; funds that are performing well need marketers to help manage new capital, and ones that are not doing well need marketers to keep assets in place. The path to getting a job as a hedge fund marketer is very different from the one to become an analyst or a trader, and that's because the job itself and the skills required are so different. Marketers must be articulate and outgoing and possess solid marketing and client service skills. Since they will be marketing the fund to potential investors while, often at the same time, keeping in contact with current investors, fund marketers also need to understand finance and be well versed in the investment strategy of the fund where they are working.

Hedge fund marketing is not the creative type of marketing often associated with other professions. There is little emphasis on producing glossy, colorful brochures or coming up with innovative advertising strategies. There is, however, a lot of client contact that must be done in a professional, articulate way, which means a lot of hedge fund marketing is about personality. It therefore shouldn't be surprising that the main entry-level marketing roles call for individuals who are talkative, social, mature, and intelligent.

While you don't have to be the life of the party, if you are not articulate and very social a fund marketing role is probably not for you. And, unlike other areas of finance, these are typically not skills that can be learned. Recruiters can usually tell within minutes of meeting someone whether marketing suits that individual's personality. It's just like the ability to sell—you either have it or you don't. Marketers are people who like to entertain and be in front of a group. If there is something that needs to be written or a speech that needs to be given, you are the one who is usually selected to handle it. And you enjoy it. You like finance and investing and are comfortable talking about those subjects, but selecting the actual investments is not your passion. You certainly don't want to construct financial models and have to check the level of the Dow Jones Industrial Average every five minutes, but you still do have a general sense of the market as a whole.

THE ROLES

There are two main roles that fall under hedge fund marketing—investor relations (IR) and fund-raising. Investor relations professionals manage relationships with existing investors, whereas fund-raisers are charged with bringing in new assets. Although there are junior IR roles, there are rarely junior fund-raising slots because people at that level do not normally have the required investor Rolodex. Some hedge funds have people who are pure IR specialists or pure fund-raisers, but at most funds the role is a blended one with one person performing both functions. In fact, it's rare that someone at a fund with less than $1 billion in assets under management would be purely IR unless a fund has closed to new investors and thus has no need for someone to do fund-raising.

As their name implies, investor relations specialists spend more time managing existing clients and their requests than raising money (that's what fund-raisers do). Investor relations professionals are charged with keeping the existing money happy. Simply put, you are the forward face of the fund.

The size of the marketing staff is usually dictated by the amount of assets under management (AUM). In a larger fund there may be a multiple-person staff that handles all marketing needs, including investor relations and fund-raising. In a smaller fund there may be one or two people who handle all of the functions. In that case the senior person would do all of the client facing work and the junior person would be charged with putting together all of the marketing materials and coordinating the dissemination of requests for proposals (RFPs) and requests for information (RFIs) received from people who are considering investing in the fund.

CAREER PATH

The traditional career path of a fund marketer begins by taking a client services role. After a few years the marketer may move on to handle investor relations and eventually, after several years of total experience, could graduate on to a fund-raising role after he/she has cultivated an investor Rolodex. In funds with $1 billion or less in AUM, the fund-raising and IR functions generally are blended into one role, and that bundled role would supervise a client service professional.

Most true junior fund marketing roles, meaning the person who is going out on meetings with investors, talking about the fund, and potentially gathering assets, require previous experience. Individuals who land this type of position have typically worked for a few years either in another marketing capacity or in a finance role. These people work closely with the head of fund-raising and are expected to build their network of contacts, as they are frequently groomed to be a fund-raiser.

ROOM FOR UNDERGRADUATES

There is a window for some individuals to get into fund marketing directly out of undergraduate school; these, however, would mainly be entry-level, junior client services positions that are more operational in nature. This role, which reports to the head of fund marketing, would handle various types of client requests, including questions about performance and assisting senior staff with fund-raising initiatives. Among other chores, individuals in this position would draft quarterly reports and annual performance updates that are distributed to investors while at the same time handling the operational/administrative side of subscriptions (if an investor wants to join the fund) and redemptions (if one wants to pull out). If successful, a junior client services person could be groomed to move into a more senior role.

POSITIONING YOURSELF

It should go without saying that you need to be mature and articulate. If you are still in college, we recommend getting an internship in a private wealth management firm, as this will give you a good foundation for dealing with affluent investors and will help you understand the types of questions these investors tend to ask. Second, we suggest getting to know a marketing professor. You'd be surprised how many professors know hedge fund managers and could possibly help get you in the door.

Regardless of where you are in your career, to work in a fund marketing capacity you should have a general interest in finance and be able to follow and understand the markets. As for personality, you should be an outgoing, people-oriented person.

Having previous marketing experience is definitely helpful, and we suggest targeting jobs in the client services or capital introduction (cap intro) groups at prime brokerages (cap intro groups introduce investors to hedge funds). Working at an investment consultant firm can also give you the necessary skills to get into hedge fund marketing. Clients of investment consultants are pension funds and other large institutional investors. Working there you would be helping them allocate their assets and would become well versed in the types of investors that may also want to invest in a hedge fund.

The big hedge funds generally have openings for junior client services roles. As you would expect, they look for people who come from a finance/marketing background. Some ideal networking groups include Hedge Funds Care, 100 Women in Hedge Funds, and 85 Broads. We'd also recommend going to industry conferences as a great way to network. As with other positions in financial services, we suggest using your alumni network.

If you are already in private wealth management, you may be ready to move to a hedge fund marketing role. If you are in investment banking and have thoughts of switching to marketing, you may have to convince a firm that you are sincere about wanting to be a marketer and don't have your sights set on moving to the investment side. Those with a background in institutional equity sales could be well positioned to land a marketing position because they probably have good rapport with clients and knowledge of the products. Another good feeder into marketing is a fund of hedge funds, even if you are an analyst. This allows the candidate to have solid knowledge of trading strategies.

The strategy(ies) used by a hedge fund can also dictate the type of experience required. In an ideal world long/short equity funds would want candidates with equity sales experience and fixed income and distressed funds would target people who have sold fixed-income products. The more complicated strategies such as statistical arbitrage and ones that use quantitative-based strategies will want someone who knows that particular strategy and perhaps has an advanced degree in mathematics. In a realistic world, however, funds usually don't get those perfect candidates so it becomes more important that they get marketers with "sales DNA" or a client services temperament.

SAMPLE JOB SEARCHES

For a glimpse of the requirements for some of the different marketing roles, we suggest you take a look at the job specifications for positions that follow. The first two listings are more junior positions, while the second two are more senior. Pay careful attention to the description of the role and the amount of experience sought for each job.

Search 1: Investor Relations Associate

Multibillion-dollar hedge fund and large fund of hedge funds
This is a typical entry-level position and is a great way to break into a hedge fund by paying your dues and learning the strategy.

Description

The investor relations associate will work closely with the firm's director of partner relations. The associate will modify and/or create marketing presentations and investor letters/correspondence. The associate will also handle any ad hoc client requests.

Requirements

- At least one year of relevant financial marketing experience.
- Undergraduate degree from a top institution.
- Energetic, motivated, and personable.
- Team player.
- Excellent verbal and written communication skills; good phone manner.
- Client service focused; ability to interact with investors.
- Attention to detail.
- Technology proficiency—Word, Excel, PowerPoint, customer relationship management (CRM) systems.
- Knowledge of and passion for financial markets.
- Ability to multitask.

Search 2: Investor Relations Associate

Multibillion-dollar New York City–based hedge fund
This could be a good position for someone looking to switch careers. Candidates from private wealth management, banking, or traditional long-only financial marketing will be considered.

Description

The fund is seeking a talented generalist associate to support all aspects of the department's activities, including fund transactional operations, marketing, structuring, and sales. The associate will have substantial contact with investors; will gain exposure to many areas of the firm, including trading, financial operations, legal, and marketing; and is expected to gradually assume additional marketing and structuring responsibilities.

Requirements

- Must have one to three years of related financial marketing experience.
- Must have undergraduate degree from a top institution with high GPA.
- Must have outstanding interpersonal, writing, and presentation skills.
- Extreme attention to detail, strong organizational skills, and the desire to excel in a dynamic work environment are essential.

Search 3: Senior Fund-Raiser

Long/short equity hedge fund
Notice the specific fund-raising qualifications and hedge fund experience desired.

Description

Our client is seeking an experienced fund-raiser to join the firm. In general, the fund-raiser will be responsible for raising assets from the high net worth and family office investing community.

Responsibilities

- Arrange for and conduct fund-raising meetings with clients and their respective investment consultants.
- Provide leadership and day-to-day management of firmwide marketing initiative.
- Create and/or redesign existing marketing literature.

Requirements

- Minimum of five years of fund-raising experience from a fund of hedge funds, hedge fund, or private client division of a large bank.
- Extensive and active high-net-worth investor Rolodex.
- Strong leadership and communication skills.
- Strong teamwork skills.
- Top-tier undergraduate degree.

Search 4: Director of Client Relations

Multibillion-dollar fundamental value hedge fund

The top candidates for this search will have both investing and fund-raising experience at a hedge fund.

Description

We seek a director of client relations who will report directly to the partners and will manage the firm's investor relations needs. Candidate will conduct marketing presentations and serve as current and prospective investors' primary point of contact for all investment issues. Candidate will also perform all investor reporting and investor maintenance with respect to Schedule K-1s, privacy notices, Form ADV distributions, and all weekly, monthly, and quarterly requests/assignments.

Requirements

- Must have at least two years of experience in investment banking or asset management and strong familiarity with principles of value investing.
- Should have at least two years of investor relations/marketing/client service administration experience.
- Must have excellent communication skills and project management skills.
- Must have strong academic background.

CASE STUDIES

To follow are the stories of two individuals who secured fund marketing positions. The first began in a private bank where she had direct exposure to hedge funds. The second person was able to land a more senior position after working on both the buy- and sell-sides in marketing capacities.

Case Study 17: A Classic Fund Marketer

This person took one of the classic routes into hedge fund marketing—beginning at a private bank. By working with high-net-worth clients and researching hedge funds she set herself up perfectly to move into a hedge fund IR role.

■ ■ ■

Although I was interested in finance and graduated with a degree in economics from an Ivy League school (class of 2002), I didn't want to go into an investment banking program—the long hours were not for me. Instead, I applied to and was accepted into a two-year internal consulting program at a bulge-bracket bank (I had done an internship with the same bank the summer after my junior year). This was a rotational program that put me in different groups every six months. The hope was that I would find my area of interest or niche within the bank by the end of the program. I spent my last rotation in the bank's private bank and was eventually placed into the private bank's Alternative Investments Group as an investor relations analyst.

Without knowing it at the time, I was laying the groundwork for a move into hedge fund marketing. In the private bank I was a member of the team that sourced, structured, and serviced alternative investment opportunities for private clients with close to $20 billion in assets under management. Personally I covered hedge, private equity, and real estate funds, giving me exposure to the entire spectrum of alternative investments. In addition to handling funds' activities and client inquiries, my responsibilities included organizing and conducting monthly due diligence calls with hedge fund managers, composing a monthly risk management report, analyzing and evaluating funds' and clients' investment performances, and working with the internal relationship managers and sales force. I enjoyed my work, the exposure I had to clients, and working as a liaison between them and the funds in which they were invested.

"My advice to any would-be fund marketers is to be patient and work toward your goal. This side of the business needs people who are very outgoing, detail-oriented, quick learners and who understand the markets."

After about two and a half years, I felt my learning curve had peaked. Although I knew things at a high level, I didn't have as much of an in-depth knowledge of the industry, the markets, and the funds as I would have liked. Given the analysis I had been doing, going to a fund of funds might have been a natural move, but I was more interested in single-manager funds and began to interview for fund marketing roles.

At the fund where I eventually got an offer I was interviewed for a fund-raising/marketing role. My first interview was with the firm's CFO and CAO (chief administrative officer). It was a very basic meeting that focused more on why I wanted to leave the private bank and why I would want to move from a large firm to a very small one. My knowledge of hedge funds was not tested. This fund focuses on the emerging markets and I was asked how I would feel about concentrating on such a small part of the overall markets.

When I returned for a second round I met with the CFO and CAO again, but was also interviewed by the firm's CEO, who is also the portfolio manager. As is common, I was asked some of the same questions as were asked during the first round. This time they also wanted to know why I wanted to be on the buy side and why I was interested in the specific country in which the fund invests. It was clear to me that they were concerned that I wouldn't feel comfortable switching from a large, global bank to a small, niche fund. They wanted to know if I am a detail-oriented person and if I work well with a team. I was also asked the classic questions: List three of your strengths and three of your weaknesses. I knew that a small firm would be very different and was ready for the challenge. Even if there was some administrative stuff that had to be done, the added responsibility and the chance to grow made it worthwhile for me.

At my last meeting, I met with the same people again and the firm's head trader (most of the investment team is based in Asia). This time it seemed they were trying to sell the job to me. This was a new position for them and they obviously wanted to make sure there was a good fit. They were in the process of reopening the fund and wanted someone to help with additional fund-raising. After accepting the position I found that I had indeed been preparing myself for this position without knowing it. I now do research on endowments and foundations, meet and call on prospective clients, and help write marketing presentations.

My advice to any would-be fund marketers is to be patient and work toward your goal. This side of the business needs people who are very outgoing, detail-oriented, quick learners and who understand the markets (in my case I was not always outgoing and sociable, but have become more confident and outgoing over time, with much of the confidence coming with my work experience). It's also important that people can intelligently and eloquently speak to clients and are able to work well with all kinds of people. In my case working at a private bank was an ideal stepping-stone to hedge funds—if someone can deal with high-net-worth investors they can pretty much deal with anybody. My firm liked that I had client contact and that I could, if necessary, deal with high-strung clients complaining about losing money. I hope I don't get any of those "Hey, the fund is down 3%—why is it down?" types of calls, but if I do I can handle them. I've found that as long as you manage clients' expectations you won't get hysterical phone calls.

Case Study 18: Moving into a Senior Role

This person had extensive sell-side experience and some traditional asset management marketing experience from a fixed income shop. She was able to translate that into a fundraising position at a small hedge fund. Note how she approached her interviews and came prepared with a lengthy presentation.

■ ■ ■

My entrance into hedge funds came after I had been working in financial services for about 12 years and, although the fund was taking a bit of a chance on me because I didn't have much experience in equity or marketing any type of hedge account, I was still able to enter in a senior fund-raising role.

My professional career began with an undergraduate degree in business administration with a concentration in management. My first job was as an institutional equity sales assistant at a small Wall Street firm. I followed that by moving into high-yield sales and high-yield strategy at a bulge-bracket bank. That job led me into my first marketing position and client service position. I did this at a high-yield shop and was responsible for bringing in $10 billion in new assets and 50 new clients. While at that firm I interacted with clients; put together presentation materials; advised the firm on client objectives, reporting requirements, and restrictions; and filled out request for proposal questionnaires for prospective accounts.

After about five years marketing high-yield products I felt the itch to move on and thought my combination of sell-side and buy-side experience would make me marketable to a hedge fund. My goal was to find a revenue-producing position, and I was willing to work hard. I was able to raise funds at my old firm through blood, sweat, and tears. It wasn't easy, but momentum also had a lot to do with it—it was the right time, and I was in the right place. I hoped that I could find the same opportunity at a hedge fund. My fund-raising background on the buy side was a significant entrée for me, though I am currently not fund-raising for a fixed income hedge fund product—we have a long equity strategy. In the end, my experience was transferable—it's a relationship business. If you are good, you can sell fixed income as well as equity, and hedge funds as well as mutual funds. You just have to know who to talk to and how to get to those decision makers.

> *"To highlight my experience, I wrote a full marketing proposal highlighting who I would target, who I knew in the industry, and what tools I worked with to market to new and potential clients."*

My interview process was pretty quick and relatively painless, which now I know is the exception (I began to seriously look into changing my position in July, found a recruiter in August, interviewed in September, and accepted the offer in late September). I worked with a recruiter and first met with three principals of the firm for about 30 minutes. This meeting was mostly conversational, and it seemed they were screening me to make sure I had the skills they needed. My next set of interviews lasted a full day at the firm's office. I first met one additional principal and then had lunch with two others and the portfolio manager. We basically talked about how I would grow the funds. I was going from a $12 billion fund to a $20 million one, so I knew I was taking a chance. They wanted to know how my experience would help them grow their fund. The hedge fund interview process, like any other industry, is familiar yet extremely strange. There are things you know will happen, and then there are things that completely catch you off guard. The point is that each process will be different, but you still have to prepare. My new portfolio manager wrote a book in the mid-1990s, which I obtained and read the weekend before my interview.

I knew my background was in fixed income, though I would be selling equity. To highlight my experience, I wrote a full marketing proposal highlighting who I would target, who I knew in the industry, and what tools I worked with to market to new and potential clients. This proposal clearly and succinctly highlighted what I could bring to the table; it quantified what I knew and how I felt my background could raise assets. This, I feel, was the major key to winning the position. I stood out from the rest of the pack—taking a chance, in some ways, because I was laying all my cards on the table. It took a while to produce, but a marketing proposal is my best recommendation. Whether you present it without distribution or you make copies for all players, it becomes the backbone of your interview process. You organize it and put down your highlighted topics; you can then somewhat steer the interview, depending on your interviewer. It then becomes a more level playing field. In writing the proposal, you get a significant chance to *think* about your accomplishments (or failures), your most challenging task, and so on, and *write* down your thoughts. A proposal gives you a guide for your interview, letting you think about your experience and the past before you head into a potential employer's office.

I would advise people interviewing for another type of position within a hedge fund to put together a similar type of proposal. You are putting down your ideas and qualifications in a format that provides clarity and guidance. I would suppose that most interview candidates do not put together such a piece; anything that you can do to stand out in a positive fashion puts you at an advantage.

As it pertains specifically to getting into marketing at a hedge fund, I would begin by reminding candidates that marketing/selling is a relationship business. The interview process often comes down to the simple fact that your potential employer likes you and just has a good feeling. You could write a 1,000-page proposal, but if your potential employer doesn't like you, or you don't like him, there is nothing that is going to make it work for the long term. Be yourself and do your best to project what you can truly and honestly bring to the table. Do not sugarcoat your abilities; they will be tested, and if you can't deliver, there will be a problem. Remember, you want to work for a certain type of company and a certain type of employer—don't compromise if you feel it's not a good fit. In the long term, it is better to wait to have an employer honestly appreciate you and your talents. There is nothing better than having a productive and long-term relationship with an employer. To this day, I still send birthday cards to the salespeople I used to work for at my former firm. If you are true to yourself and honest about your own ambitions, that will come through.

See Resume H in Appendix B on page 170.

Chapter VII

RISK MANAGEMENT

Another essential, though less glamorous, group that plays a part in the success of a hedge fund is risk management. This chapter discusses the role of risk management professionals–think of them as an internal police force that keeps tabs on the fund's activities– and the backgrounds and skills needed to land a job. To emphasize what hedge funds look for when hiring risk professionals, we thought it would be especially useful to present some actual job specifications from recent searches we worked on (you will find these toward the middle of the chapter).

In addition to analysts, traders, and marketers, most hedge funds need people, or groups of people, whose sole purpose is to monitor the fund's risk. As we've explained, hedge funds can take long and short positions in different markets and may use leverage in making their investments. All of that can make them risky and means they need specialized people to help measure and control the risks they take.

As a group within a hedge fund, risk management has evolved from a cost center that was stuck in the back office or handled on an outsourced basis—Barra, RiskMetrics, and Algorithmics are three of the leading companies to which risk functions are outsourced—to a legitimate front-office business. Many multibillion-dollar

 Glocap Insight

In a more conservative hedge fund in which the mandate is to have only a certain amount of risk, the risk management professionals are there to constantly maintain that level of risk and to make sure the portfolio managers and investment committee are aware of the fund's level of risk. If the style of the fund is one that takes more risk, then the risk management team is there to quantify that risk.

This is a fully built-out risk management group within a large hedge fund. Most funds do not have such an intricate structure. Some medium-sized funds may have only one branch of the diagram, and that could be headed by a risk manager. Some smaller funds may have one to three risk professionals, and a very small one may have only one person dedicated to risk.

Figure 7.1 Organizational Chart: Risk Management

hedge funds now have groups dedicated to risk management, and individuals working in those areas are seen as quasi-investment professionals—they help build portfolios and thus can add to a hedge fund's bottom line.

The size of a hedge fund's risk management group is correlated more to the amount and number of products the fund has and its investment style than to how much capital it has under management. For example, from what we've seen, a straightforward long/short fund can function with one or two risk professionals. On the flip side, however, a multiproduct fund may need a risk specialist for each of its different products—equity, structured products, fixed income, derivatives, mortgage-backed securities, swaps, futures, and so on. We know of one multiproduct fund that has 12 people in its risk group. Another long/short fund with $6 billion in assets under management has just two risk pros. Candidates looking to join a risk group should research the different types of hedge funds and the various strategies they employ. (For a look at an organizational chart of a fully built-out risk management group see Figure 7.1.)

To be sure, not all hedge funds have in-house risk management groups. In fact, many funds have only one person dedicated to assessing risk. Some smaller funds may use a software package to monitor their risk, while others may outsource the risk management role to a third-party vendor or receive risk management services from their prime broker.

Most risk professionals who make the switch from investment banks or buy-side firms are moving from being one of many people in a large group to one of just a few in a small group, and hedge funds will want to know that they can do the job.

RISK HIERARCHY

Some of the titles you will hear are director of risk management, risk associate, risk analyst, quantitative analyst, risk programmer, quantitative programmer, and risk manager. (See Table 7.1.) All of these people work hand in hand with investment professionals at the fund. As you would imagine, these jobs tend to be very quantitative in nature.

Table 7.1 Roles of Risk Professionals

TITLE	ROLE
Director of Risk Management	The architect for a firm's risk management infrastructure; in charge of educating the fund's investment professionals on how to read and understand risk management data; manages the risk management team and maps out any initiatives that would benefit the firm.
Risk Analyst/Risk Manager	Works hand in hand with the investment professionals and, based on their analysis, makes recommendations on how to streamline the risks that the fund takes. Also performs exposure analysis on fund portfolios.
Risk Programmer	Uses software programs to help risk managers and investment professionals analyze portfolio data while also developing back-end programs that interact directly with portfolio analysis.

ROOM FOR UNDERGRADUATES

The risk groups at hedge funds may hire candidates directly out of college or with minimal work experience. In such cases they target people who were programmers in college or who have done summer internships at financial institutions. While they are not directly investing, these people typically get excited about the public markets.

Over the years, we have seen risk professionals from investment banks make the switch to hedge funds. Many feel hedge funds are an opportunity to get closer to the action. The feeling is that at banks the risk groups are often in a separate office secluded away from the trading floor and have little interaction, if any at all, with portfolio managers and upper management. At a hedge fund, risk professionals are closer to the trading desk, and many believe they can make more of a difference. Many also make the switch for lifestyle reasons.

FUND OF FUNDS

Due to their style of investing, a fund of hedge funds usually employs larger risk teams than single-manager hedge funds. A fund of funds invests in different hedge funds, which in turn invest in different types of securities. This large range of securities raises the need for additional risk specialists. In addition to risk professionals who quantify the risk of the portfolios of the hedge funds in which the fund of funds invests, fund of funds also have operational risk managers. These professionals may physically inspect a hedge fund to examine its operations, its compliance with the Securities and Exchange Commission, how its portfolio managers and traders interact, and what types of accounting and information technology (IT) systems it uses.

The operational risk manager takes a more macro approach to monitoring risk, but the role is equally important.

CAREER PATH

Unlike other roles in a hedge fund, the career path for risk professionals is generally limited to the risk group. If you join as a risk professional, the chances of moving on to become an investment analyst are slim, as the skills and scope of work are very dissimilar. Risk associates can be promoted within to become a risk manager, make a lateral move to another fund, or return to an investment bank, insurance company, or another financial services firm.

POSITIONING YOURSELF

Most people who work in risk management groups have a degree in engineering, mathematics, statistics, and/or computer science. In short, they're engineers who are savvy in finance and have a high degree of professionalism. If you are at all interested in this role, our first piece of advice would be to make sure you possess basic quantitative skills such as knowledge of Excel and computer languages such as Structured Query Language (SQL) and Visual Basic for Applications (VBA). You should also have a basic understanding of finance and familiarity with products such as derivatives, options, swaps, and various structured products. The more senior-level risk professionals all have postgraduate degrees. These can be in financial engineering, computational mathematics, econometrics, or others.

If you aren't already, you will eventually have to become familiar with the Greeks, as options traders often refer to the delta, gamma, vega, and theta of their positions. These give traders a way to measure the sensitivity of an option's price to quantifiable factors and can help better understand the risk and potential reward of an option position. Being a good communicator is a must, because risk managers are responsible for translating complicated risk assessments into a language that portfolio managers can understand.

From our experience, the prime breeding grounds for risk professionals are risk groups at insurance companies, banks, and other large financial services firms. Another

Glocap Insight   Our own rough estimates are that 15% of the risk managers hired into hedge funds come from insurance companies, 40% from financial services firms, 20% from vendors, and the remainder from various places, including other hedge funds, energy companies, and some pure programming people.

popular source of candidates is the vendors that supply risk monitoring programs (this is especially common when someone from a vendor is working to show a hedge fund how to use its system).

A large percentage of risk hires are carried out by search firms; thus we suggest you get in touch with one that specializes in hedge funds and has placed risk professionals before. We should add that risk managers are also a very clubby sort and recommend that you get involved with industry groups and trade associations such as the Professional Risk Managers' International Association (PRMIA).

As part of your preparation, you should brush up on your programming skills, because programming is an integral component of any risk position. Like other hedge fund candidates, you should learn about the different trading strategies, as each has its own level of inherent risk. If you are not familiar with the different financial instruments, we suggest getting to know them. In interviews you will certainly be asked which instruments are you comfortable with—equities? Credit? And you should have an answer.

Although by their nature risk jobs are very quantitative and technical, hedge funds will still want to know that your personality fits with the personalities of the other professionals at the firm. In most hedge funds, risk professionals sit on the trading floor alongside traders and other investment professionals, heightening the need for a good personality fit.

SAMPLE JOB SEARCHES

To further illustrate what hedge funds look for when hiring various types of risk managers, we thought it would be helpful to include some job specifications from actual searches.

Search 1: Hedge Fund Risk Analyst

Note: This fund has a director of risk management who is looking for an additional resource (risk analyst) to join his team and develop within the firm.

Description

- Responsible for periodic report production, including:
  - Value at risk (VaR) and volatility reporting by portfolio.
  - Back-testing and historical performance measurement.
  - Portfolio segmentation analysis.
  - Factor analysis reporting.
- Position level:
  - Expected return by position.
  - Risk analysis by position.
  - Marginal impact.
  - Relative risk/reward performance:
    - Stress testing.

- Correlation and concentration reporting by name, sector, and industry.
- Responsible for the development and maintenance of a risk management database:
  - Creation of a centralized risk management database repository.
  - Daily data extraction from trading systems (Eze Castle) and accounting systems (VPM).
  - Maintenance of a security master and entity master tables.
  - Sourcing and storage of market pricing information.
  - Data cleaning and standardization.
  - Automation of data feeds from the risk management database to other applications (e.g., RiskMetrics) or models.
- Supporting portfolio analysis:
  - Position and portfolio volatility analysis.
  - Correlation and factor model development.
  - Relative risk-adjusted performance measurement.
  - Historical and prospective analysis.
  - Analysis by position, portfolio, strategy, and so on.
  - Ad hoc analysis of portfolio.

Requirements

- Two to four years of experience in financial services.
- Strong analytic background (engineering, sciences, mathematics, finance, economics).
- Knowledge of finance, statistics, risk management, database management, and linear algebra useful.
- Computer skills: Excel, SQL/Open Database Connectivity (ODBC) query construction, Visual Basic (VB), Mathematica, SQL Server, RiskMetrics.

Search 2: Risk Analyst Programmer/Quant

This hedge fund was upgrading its front office/risk technology and was looking for a candidate with excellent knowledge of performance, risk, and specifically interfaces between risk/performance and other front office/external systems.

Description

Application knowledge of RiskMetrics/Barra would be useful. You will also need good all-around front office experience and instrument knowledge of equities, fixed income securities, and derivatives. Technical skills in Microsoft technologies (e.g., VB), SQL Server, Java, JavaServer Pages (JSP), and especially SQL are desirable, as are strong project management skills. You will also need a strong personality and the ability to manage relationships with high-level business users.

CASE STUDIES

The stories that follow show two different people—one was a more junior risk hire and the other joined as a director of risk management. Both had finance skills, were especially adept at mathematics, and were proficient with the specific software programs used by the industry.

Case Study 19: Switching from the Sell Side

This case is that of a typical risk manager hire—someone with programming abilities, an interest in finance, and solid number-crunching skills.

■ ■ ■

I knew I wanted to do something on the business side after completing a double major in computer science and economics and was thinking about finance even though I didn't really know much about it and certainly had no idea what trading was about. I ended up joining a buy-side firm that recruited on campus and had an operations/tech training program in London. I came back to the United States after two months and did a one-year rotation in the alternative investments group, which, luckily for me, wasn't a true back-office job and put me in front of hedge funds. I spent four years there writing profit and loss (P&L), holdings, and risk reports; running data analytics; and doing some Web programming and scripting. I was also put on a fund of funds project where I did monthly trade reports and worked on a liquidity reporting system.

At this point I looked ahead and thought I would like to be a portfolio manager and that being a risk manager would point me in the right direction. I also wanted to see what the sell side would be like, so I joined the fixed income group of a bulge-bracket firm, where I was supporting the structured finance team. It was at this point that I realized that I definitely wanted to go to a hedge fund. A lot of colleagues had gone to hedge funds, and I knew they were more financially rewarding, there were more responsibilities, the hours were better, and, because they were smaller, there would be less politics. I also wanted to go back to the buy side. I first tried to get an investment job, but with my lack of experience in a pure business role this proved to be near impossible; so when the opportunity came up for a risk position, I was very interested because I thought it would combine my quantitative/tech skill set with finance. This way I could leverage my IT experience within a new role that was closer to my ultimate goal.

I'd say to be a risk manager someone would need a good quant background and a degree in either engineering, a hard science, or math. There is a lot of number crunching and stress testing using models, and a lot of analytics and technology work. Communication skills are also very important, as there is a lot of interaction with investors and portfolio managers. I've found that a lot of hedge funds are expanding their risk groups. This not only appeals to a wider set of investors, but allows the funds to achieve their target total returns while also striving for minimum portfolio volatility.

I went through four rounds of interviews before I got an offer. The first interview lasted about an hour and mostly focused on the position and what I wanted to do. I was asked a few brainteasers to see that I could think quantitatively. One thing that I would caution about brainteasers is that if you say the answer right away it will be obvious that you already knew that particular one. It's better if you tell them, because they want to see how you think through the question. The second round was more brainteasers and thinking puzzles. I was given an hour to do 10 of these problems. Personally, I like brainteasers so I didn't mind. Of the 10 I was given I had seen three before. In the third round I met other analysts, the CFO, and the head of investor relations. All of these meetings were conversational and were designed to get a feel for personality and whether I would fit in with the corporate culture. In the final round I met the head of the hedge fund, who gave me a verbal offer on the spot.

"Even in a position like this I'd say you can't be all techy, so people should be personable. People at the hedge fund will want to sense your energy and eagerness to do the work."

The best way to get ready for the interviews would be to practice brainteasers—remember they are complicated problems that have an easy solution. Just train your brain to think the right way. Knowing data systems, Excel, and SQL is also important.

My advice to others would be to try and get into a risk position at an investment bank right away after graduating from college. I have also heard of some hedge funds that do bring people on straight out of undergraduate school, and in this case they would target people with engineering and computer science degrees and people who have taken business, finance, and mathematics classes (math was a weakness in me that this hedge fund was willing to overlook). In math I'd say to focus on linear algebra, advanced calculus, matrix algebra, statistics, and probability theory. Even in a position like this I'd say you can't be all techy, so people should be personable. People at the hedge fund will want to sense your energy and eagerness to do the work. Hedge funds are small and collegial and you won't be tucked away in a corner doing your work, so the people will want someone whom they enjoy working with.

See Resume I in Appendix B on page 171.

Case Study 20: Taking a Roundabout Route to Risk

This person followed a more circuitous path to his role. He was a philosophy major who benefited from an ideal internship while he was in business school. In addition to having a thirst for finance, he had solid knowledge of programming, probability, and applied math.

■ ■ ■

My background was far from typical compared to others who got into finance and even risk management. I graduated in 1997 from a small liberal arts college on the West Coast with a degree in philosophy. In addition to my philosophy studies, I had a computing background.

I eventually joined an Internet start-up as, of all things, a secretary. I didn't mind taking the role, as I knew I would be helping to solve everyday problems and that it could lead into something bigger and better. After about six months I became product marketing manager and served as a liaison between the technical people and executive management. Thereafter, I worked at five different Internet companies of varying sizes over the course of five years. Some of these were small start-ups while others were larger public companies, and I held various front-office positions.

After five years working in technology I decided to take a year off and travel around Europe. While my Internet jobs had been successful, they never felt like a lifelong career, and when I was away I thought about what I really wanted to do. It needed to be something more intellectual. Through reading, I found a lot of people in finance interested in philosophy and mathematics and discovered a kinship between the two fields. There are, of course, highly quantitative aspects to finance, whether those are derivatives, risk management, or black box trading models. However, predicting the future has elements of more game theory or philosophy. I had a friend who worked at a large asset management firm, and he got me to read up on the academic literature and persuaded me to begin work on my CFA.

Through the public jobs function on Bloomberg, I got a nonpaying internship at a $50 million distressed debt fund. This was 2002 and was an interesting time for distressed debt—the sagas of WorldCom, Adelphia, and Nortel kept us busy. I had never put together an accounting or free cash flow model in my life, and it took a few days at first. But I have a good focus for details and liked creative investigation of tiny details. By the end of the year I could complete a first-pass model for a new company in a day, and, more important, I felt my appreciation of "quality of earnings" type analysis was good. The fund finished the year down a few single digits and was considering closing. That made it easy for me to walk away.

By now I had finished Level 1 of my CFA and had begun business school on a part-time basis. I thought getting an MBA would be a good move for someone looking to transition careers. In the spring of 2003 I got a paid internship reporting to the global head of market risk at a bulge-bracket investment bank. The position had been posted on a rival business school jobs board. I didn't know that much about risk, but was definitely interested in the financial markets in a broad way. Coming off of my last role I was still in a hedge fund state of mind where you want to take risk and had to get used to how sell-side firms operate and approach risk—where traders at sell-side firms may want to take risks, but it is generally in the firm's interest to hold them back.

My initial internship, which paid me by the hour, evolved into a full-time role in which I was part of a 30-person team charged with monitoring the firm's risk. This position gave me a great education in finance, even more so than my CFA and MBA programs. I was exposed to, and learned, all types of financial instruments including equity, fixed income, derivatives, equity-linked instruments, leases, collateralized and structured trades, and so on. My final year at the firm I worked for the chief institutional strategist on fixed income trading and research. We did risk consulting for large financial institutions to facilitate derivatives trades and other structuring business opportunities across the firm.

After three years, I decided it was time for me to move on. Ever since my previous work experience at the distressed debt fund I had been interested in returning to another hedge fund and was hoping firms would look past my unorthodox background. I was interested in investing and the risk-taking side of the business. I decided to pursue both risk management positions and investment analyst ones, but I focused on the latter at smaller or start-up shops. I hadn't done any investing in the public markets—either on my own or in a professional capacity—but I'm a firm believer in the applied intelligence theory: Anyone who is intelligent (and has creativity and common sense) can bring those tools to profit in financial instruments. I also thought I would have the most upside at smaller, one- or two-person funds.

Working through a recruiter, I was sent on some interviews and was eventually hired as the director of risk management at a multibillion-dollar fund. While I have a diverse background, I know I am very competitive. I easily passed the CFA. I was a top student in my graduate finance and mathematical finance courses. I knew that risk management was what I had been doing, so it was a good place to elevate my career.

"How could you say you are interested in risk at a hedge fund without knowing the products used?"

During the interviews, I felt I hit it off immediately with the investment professionals and maybe can attribute that to the combination of a good academic finance foundation with a practical approach that is rare in quants or risk managers. I might also credit my generalist background, which also seems to be quite rare. As with other hedge funds, I had to meet almost everyone at the firm. In the first round I met the firm's COO, one portfolio manager, and an administrator. In the next round, I met the CFO, a few traders, a couple more portfolio managers, and the head of the firm. At the beginning, most of the questions focused on personality and fit. We talked about what I saw as the role of risk management at the firm, how to build infrastructure, and short- and long-term goals. We spoke a lot about finance, but this was no problem for me. In fact, I love talking about finance so I always find those discussions enjoyable. Risk management is still in the build-out phase at hedge funds, so there aren't too many people who have been doing it and I had a number of my own ideas.

In the end, I really enjoy the business and think it fits the way my brain works. I plan to have a good time making a fortune in my own investment firm someday. I believe this firm saw the strength within a developing background and someone who had a hard-to-find combination of generalist risk experience along with enough quantitative knowledge to have detailed thoughts on the use of risk management in a long/short equity hedge fund. Of course, I had come a decent way in the career transition—CFA, MBA, four years of tough low-pay experience.

My advice to any would-be risk analysts or programmers would be to read a lot. In addition to the classics such as Peter Bernstein's *Against the Gods: The Remarkable Story of Risk*, the basic academic texts should be required reading: Tuchman's *Fixed-Income Securities* and Hull's *Futures and Options*. I've interviewed PhDs for risk positions who haven't read the basics about bonds and other financial instruments. How could you say you are interested in risk at a hedge fund without knowing the products used? Beyond books and academic articles, there is a great wealth of professional writing that is widely available (www.gloriamundi.org), various blogs, and research put out by PIMCO and other investment firms. If you can't get access to these, have your friends print them out for you in exchange for a beer and a steak! Excel is still the bread and butter of everything a risk professional does. I would also advise becoming familiar with the slightly more advanced tools within Excel such as pivot tables and lookups. Knowledge of simple database programming and having a good sense of probability and applied math (very rare) are also important skills to have.

See Resume J in Appendix B on page 172.

Chapter VIII

OPERATIONS

As hedge funds have evolved, so, too, has their infrastructure. In today's market, more and more hedge funds are performing their own back office functions, and this has created opportunities for individuals with (and sometimes without) operations backgrounds.

Operations is an integral but often overlooked department within hedge funds. Although some hedge funds outsource their operations functions, there is a distinct move to bring more of these activities in-house (partly because many funds believe outside administrators are not providing a satisfactory level of service). And even the funds that outsource still need in-house operations professionals to work with the outside service providers and prime brokers.

THE ROLES

In most hedge funds, the operations functions are generally run by the chief operating officer (COO). The COO, in turn, typically oversees the following individuals to the extent they exist at a specific fund: the director of operations, operations managers, operations specialists, and traders' assistants, who work closely with individual traders. In-house operations professionals correspond on a daily basis with the fund's legal, compliance, risk management, and, at times, investor relations professionals. Some of the specific tasks they are responsible for are:

- Settling and uploading trades.
- Corporate actions and reconciliations.
- Creating and maintaining new reports.
- Reporting, reconciliation, settlement, and confirmation process.
- Liaising with relevant traders on all trade-related issues.

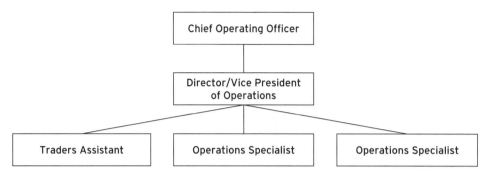

The organization of a hedge fund's operations group depends on the size of the fund. Larger funds will have multiple specialists working under the director of operations. A smaller fund may have only one internal person dedicated to operations, and that person could have a bigger title such as vice president of operations or operations manager.

Figure 8.1   Organizational Chart: Operations

- Working closely with the risk department, portfolio managers, and traders.
- Overseeing portfolio pricing, analysis, and reporting.

More advanced responsibilities may include:

- Building a firm's proprietary risk measures around its own portfolio management system.
- Monitoring in-house models that value and track investments.
- Designing reports to satisfy compliance requirements.
- Managing portfolio pricing issues.
- For a fund of funds, performing operational due diligence on underlying funds.
- In many cases COOs are overseeing all noninvestment functions.

Working in the operations department of a hedge fund is a good way for someone who does not have investment skills to get exposure to investing (for example, an operations specialist at a long/short fund may be involved in valuation work). Unlike sell-side firms (and most traditional long-only asset management firms), where the back-office functions may be housed in a satellite facility, at a hedge fund the operations professionals often sit alongside the fund's researchers, traders, risk managers, and compliance professionals and therefore can feel more like part of the overall team. (For a look at an operations group at a hedge fund, see Figure 8.1.)

POSITIONING YOURSELF

When looking to hire operations professionals, hedge funds often turn to the obvious pool of talent—their own prime brokers and fund administrators (these are the firms to which hedge funds outsource their operations). Hiring firms generally prefer people with undergraduate degrees in finance or accounting and high overall GPAs. We've also seen operations professionals hired from other hedge funds and investment banks.

Although pedigree is not as important, funds will pay close attention to undergraduate and graduate school GPAs and SAT scores and want to see excellence in both areas. In addition to academics, hedge funds look for specific product knowledge and will pay up for experience in the more sophisticated products such as derivatives, credit default swaps (CDS), collateralized debt obligations (CDOs), and collateralized loan obligations (CLOs).

As with other hedge fund roles, it's good to know the different hedge fund investment strategies. Hedge funds can be extremely picky when hiring, so whatever you can do to differentiate yourself and show you have additional skills will be helpful. We strongly suggest being very well versed in industry-specific systems. For example, if you are working in trade support or accounting you should get to know Advent/Axys, and if you are working with equities you will want to be proficient in trade support systems such as Eze Castle. Knowledge of Visual Basic (VB) programming and Excel are also important skills to have.

If you are currently in operations at an investment bank, we recommend doing what you can to learn more about the products you are working with. For example, if you focus on interest rate derivatives, in addition to being able to explain the operations side of those products, you should understand how they work. If you can do that you should be able to separate yourself from other candidates applying for hedge fund positions.

Unfortunately, hedge funds are not known to teach operations processes and skills and, therefore, it's rare that they will hire someone with no operations experience (Case Study 22 is an exception to that rule, but that person benefited from a strong family contact). To be qualified for an operations position, we recommend first getting a position in operations in an investment bank or a fund administrator. If you are hired for one of those positions, you should try for a role that will give you the most hands-on experience with products—the more complex the better. You don't want to be simply reconciling accounts. From our experience, working in operations at a hedge fund can potentially be a stepping-stone to a position on the investment side, although this is not common.

SAMPLE JOB SEARCHES

To better understand what hedge funds look for when hiring for operations positions, take a look at these four job searches, paying close attention to the job specifications and responsibilities.

Search 1: Operations Associate

Responsibilities

- Produce daily P&L and leverage reports that are distributed to partners and trading desk.
- Analyze foreign exchange exposures and provide consolidated trades to desk for execution.

- Interact with senior traders and analysts on pricing, P&L, and reorganization issues.
- Review all CDS trade confirmations and be able to flag potential issues regarding termination events or events of default.
- Step into daily settlements role to assist with basic prime brokerage issues—trade breaks, fails, and margin.
- Complete ad hoc projects as needed.

Requirements

Must have:

- Two to five years of operations/accounting experience.
- Derivatives experience and detailed knowledge about derivatives especially credit default swaps and documents required by the International Swaps and Derivatives Association (ISDA).
- Exceptional math and communication skills.
- Extremely detail-oriented, with the ability to multitask and prioritize.
- Top academic credentials.

Search 2: Trade Operations Analyst

Responsibilities

- Resolve all trade-related breaks on a daily basis for all products (OTC, listed, and other derivatives products).
- Monitor and report on all trade exceptions and trade fails on a daily basis.
- Monitor and control all trade allocations for all the funds.
- Reconcile all discrepancies to effectively run EOD process.
- Create management reports to track efficiencies.
- Oversee and maximize prime brokerage relationships from an operations support and technology perspective.
- Participate in continuing education programs and remain current on all applicable operational matters.
- Participate in the development of procedures and systems to consolidate all pertinent information to perform all the preceding tasks.
- Identify redundancies and suggest improvements in the existing process.

Requirements

- One to three years of relevant experience in trade ops or middle office, with a history of reconciling, monitoring, and fixing trades and trade-related breaks.
- Proficiency in Microsoft Excel and Microsoft Word.

- Knowledge of Oasys, CTM, Bloomberg, Eze Castle, and Geneva helpful.
- Preferably some experience in each of the following products:
  - International and domestic equities.
  - International and domestic bonds.
  - Credit derivatives.
  - Equity swaps.
- Understanding of DTC and DTCC settlement.

Search 3: Loan Operations Associate

Description

The position would allow a successful candidate to become completely knowledgeable about the operational aspects of the leveraged loan and high-yield bond markets, as well as about securitized investment vehicles (CLOs/CDOs). Familiarity with syndicated loans and a working knowledge of Wall Street Office (WSO) (or comparable loan administration software) would be ideal but are not expressly required.

Responsibilities

- Coordinate the execution and settlement of all trades and reconcile all trade breaks with counterparties.
- Update systems and Excel spreadsheets with investment/cash activity (i.e., interest and principal payments, rollovers, rate resets, new borrowings, restructurings, etc.).
- Reconcile cash accounts with trustee and prepare daily cash reports.
- Analyze and summarize all investment restructurings/refinancings.
- Resolve any bank reconciliation/safekeeping differences.
- Conduct extensive interaction with finance team, investment team, and outside counsel.
- Address all inquiries/requests within a reasonable time frame.
- Perform periodic compliance testing.

Requirements

- Bachelor's degree with one to seven years of industry or equivalent experience.
- Must possess a working knowledge of Microsoft Excel (WSO a plus).
- Accounting knowledge preferred.
- Excellent verbal and written communication skills.
- Proven ability to work in a fast-paced team-oriented environment.
- Strong prioritization and organizational skills.
- Must be diligent and meticulous.
- Willing to work additional hours when necessary.

Search 4: Trading Assistant

Note: This fund invests in event-driven, risk arbitrage and distressed opportunities. The fund was seeking an "extremely bright and hungry" person who is willing to learn in a fast-paced environment. This person would perform tasks such as booking trades and analyzing risk.

Requirements

- Undergraduate degree from a top institution, with a record of academic achievement.
- At least one to two years of experience in the financial services sector.
- High level of maturity and entrepreneurial zeal, with the ability to thrive in a faster-paced, less structured environment.
- Must be hardworking, genuinely interested in investing, and able to work in a team environment.

CASE STUDIES

The following are case studies of two people who landed positions in the operations groups of hedge funds. The first person took a more traditional route by first working in the back office of a sell-side firm. The second person was fortunate to get in the door via a close family contact. Both hope their operations roles will be a means to get into the investment side of the business.

Case Study 21: The Basic Ops Hire

This person had the ideal background to land an operations position—he held two back-office positions, and in one he interfaced with hedge funds. Although his role is definitely operations, he has been told there is a possibility he could grow into an investment position.

■ ■ ■

Although I grew up in the United States, I graduated from a small university in Canada (class of 2004), where I studied economics and humanities. I was thinking about a career in finance, but found that getting into a two-year analyst program was tough without an Ivy League degree.

I decided to work in my father's company for a few months, and then I got a temporary job as a trade accountant in the corporate actions department of a major sell-side firm. This was a typical back-office position in which I processed trades, worked with brokers and traders to transfer and settle bonds and mutual funds, and performed audits on funds. I didn't know it at the time, but this position was teaching me the skills that would help me break into a hedge fund.

After several months at this job, I felt it was time to move on. A few friends had moved to New York City and had room for me in their apartment. I took them up on their offer and began to search for a job. I landed another temporary position that soon became permanent in the back office of a major Wall Street firm. This position gave me my first direct exposure to alternative assets, as I was working on fund management for hedge funds and alternative investment companies. I handled all the daily activities (trading, repricings, reconciliations, etc.) for six major debt funds. After about 10 months I knew I wanted to try to work at a hedge fund. I had been investing on my own since I graduated from college and even did some day trading—it showed me that it wasn't as hard to make money as I had thought it was. I began working with a recruiter and going on interviews. My initial goal was to work as an analyst at a fund of hedge funds, but soon found out that I lacked the requisite experience of conducting due diligence on fund managers (not many people do, but the fund at which I interviewed wanted someone to step in and hit the ground running). I tried getting into an analyst program, but had no luck again.

"Even though I didn't want to be pigeonholed as a back-office person, I began to realize that operations would be the way for me to get in the door."

Even though I didn't want to be pigeonholed as a back-office person, I began to realize that operations would be the way for me to get in the door. The interview process for back-office positions is very different than it is for research analysts. At the firm where I eventually got an offer, my first (and only) meeting began with a managing director and the firm's head trader, who talked with me about the firm, its new debt products, and how it operated as a close-knit group of individuals. The meeting ended up lasting for two and a half hours, during which time I met with the vice president and the president of the operations group, another managing director who was head of human resources and new product development, and also one of the firm's founders. It seemed that from my work experience they were confident I could do the job I was being interviewed for. Most of the questions were personality ones, and the overall tone was very laid-back. I was not grilled on anything to do with operations. In a way they were selling me more on the firm and the position than interviewing me. I was expected to be able to come in and help create efficiencies with respect to how this firm could run its operations better. After about 10 days, the firm took me out to lunch and offered me the job. I was hired to be the fourth member of the operations team, working on fund management, day-to-day trade activity, and cash settlements.

My advice to anyone looking to break into hedge funds would be to understand that there are more than just research and trading positions. Without us (operations professionals), traders wouldn't be able to do their job. I'm still hopeful that one day I can move to the investment side. This firm didn't guarantee it, but they also said the possibility is there. At my firm the analysts work late, and I've already asked if I could stay and work with them to see what they are doing. Of course I was told yes, and I think that showed them that I want to learn. Working in operations requires attention to detail. You've got to want to create efficiencies and streamline processes and enjoy that challenge. Math skills are very useful, as are being highly competent in Excel and being able to communicate effectively. This is not like a back office at an investment bank where you are away from the action. Here we sit with analysts and traders and interact with them.

If I could do it all over again I probably would not take time off after college working with my father. I enjoyed it, but I think my time could have been better spent doing more research into finding the right job for me. Still, I'm very happy where I ended up. I definitely see operations as a possible entry into the investment side of the business and will continue to work toward that.

See Resume K in Appendix B on page 173.

Case Study 22: Straight out of Undergraduate School

This person used a family contact to get in the door of an up-and-coming hedge fund. After spending a few years at one fund, he moved on to another where he may have the opportunity to eventually move to the investment side.

■ ■ ■

Although I majored in finance (small New England school), I had a hard time getting interviews as a senior because I lacked solid internships. I participated in ROTC so my summers were tied up. That put me at a disadvantage compared to my classmates. I was always good at math and was thinking about a career in finance, but was definitely not thinking hedge funds. I ended up taking a few months off after college and began my search in the fall after I graduated.

I was able to get a few interviews and was well into the process for a credit analyst position at one bulge-bracket firm. Unfortunately, the person with whom I was interviewing was in the Reserves and he was called to Iraq. That basically brought that interview to a halt. Luckily for me, a family friend who knew what had happened sent my resume to the COO of an up-and-coming hedge fund. This fund was looking to fill an operations role. I didn't know much about operations, but I knew how rare it is for someone to get into a hedge fund straight out of college. And, given this particular fund, this seemed like an amazing opportunity. I immediately bought some hedge fund career guides and learned as much as I could about the industry, the different investment styles, and how hedge funds work.

I went through three rounds of interviews. My interviewers knew full well that I didn't have the relevant experience, so the questions were more an assessment of my personality traits. They wanted to know such things as whether I could think out of the box and could work well with the team that was in place. I was also asked some basic finance questions and about what I wanted to get out of the job, such as: Do you understand how options work? Do you know what merger arbitrage entails? What do you know about hedge funds? What is attractive about working at a hedge fund? For the last, I knew not to say the chance to make a lot of money. Instead, I acknowledged how rare an opportunity it is to come straight out of college and work at a buy-side shop and how I would make the most of it. I spoke about how interested I was in investing and the markets and that I enjoyed working with numbers.

In all, I had three rounds of interviews. In the first I met with the direct person who was hiring and then two other managers. They began with basic finance/technical questions. As the interview progressed the questions morphed more into why *I* thought the role would be a good fit for me and I would be a good fit for them. The second round came two days later. I met with a senior-level manager and the COO, who asked me many of the same questions. This is something you have to get used to—being asked the same questions over and over again and answering them without seeming like you are frustrated. One hurdle I had to get over was my lack of experience. This put me in the position of having to sell myself. I remember being asked point-blank, "What is it about you that should make me hire you when I can take the same amount of money, or just a little more, and get someone with experience?" I spoke about being a team player and being independent. I pointed out my passion for investing and that I had gotten good grades in my finance courses. I guess I did a good job, because the third round was a meeting with the firm's executive recruiter, immediately after which I was extended an offer.

As a middle-office analyst I monitored daily trade activity, worked on trade settlements, and performed daily cash reconciliations and position reconciliations to the prime brokers and fund administrator. As I learned more I performed daily net asset value (NAV) publishing as well as month-end accounting and NAV reporting for investors, conducted month-end reconciliations, and handled trial balance and income statement production. I gained exposure to a variety of products, including equities, over-the-counter (OTC) equity derivatives, foreign exchange (FX) options, FX forwards, futures, options, corporate bonds, and many others. I also became proficient in Eze Castle, Advent Geneva and Axys, Bloomberg, and Microsoft Excel operating systems.

Although I had taken on some senior responsibilities such as running the operations for this firm's overseas office, helping with the development of risk-analytic spreadsheets for the portfolio managers, assisting with the selection and negotiation of new prime broker agreements for new accounts, and helping to select and train the future operational team for the office, after about two and a half years at this firm there were some management changes and cost cutting and I felt it was time to move on. I wanted to move to the front office and into more of a trading role and knew it would not happen at this firm. I worked with a recruiter who put me in touch with a few firms that had openings, but I was shut out due to my age and relative inexperience. Finally, I interviewed for a traders assistant position at a well-known hedge fund. At this firm this role was more like that of a junior trader. The head of trading had three assistants and he didn't want to deal with questions from the back office and prime brokers. He wanted somebody who knew operations and how to support traders. That made me ideally suited for the role. I also knew the exact same trading system that this firm used. In exchange for someone who was basically plug-and-play, the firm was willing to let me learn trading.

From what I've seen, anyone still in college who wants to work at a hedge fund should get some good summer internships. These will help you build your network, which is very important. It isn't very likely that you will get an analyst or trading position straight out of school—even if you are an Ivy Leaguer with a 4.0 GPA. So, it becomes more who you know coming out of college than what you know. I was lucky to get where I did thanks to the help of a very close family friend. I'd also say that spending a few years in an investment banking program is a good idea. It's almost like another level of school and can teach you a lot about how Wall Street works. Having gotten where I am today I wouldn't have changed the path I took to get here, but I know that my resume would have been stronger if I had a few years on the sell side.

> *"At a hedge fund the ops people are not just faces in the crowd. You sit with the traders and analysts and therefore have more face time with them and more exposure to the senior people."*

Working in the back office has its pluses and minuses. The money may not be as good in the beginning, but there is a definite career path and you can work your way up to COO or CFO. At those levels the money can be good and may even be more stable than it is for people on the investment side. As a trader/analyst you have more risk that a bad year can set your compensation back. If a trader has two bad years, it might be hard for him to explain that on his resume. My resume will always have my operations experience. If trading doesn't work out for me, I can always go back to the ops side.

I'd say that young people should not discount the value of working in operations. Working in ops is a great way to learn how the entire hedge fund works. That would never happen on the sell side, where you might be secluded at an off-site location and may be totally focused on settling one particular type of security. At a hedge fund the ops people are not just faces in the crowd. You sit with the traders and analysts and therefore have more face time with them and more exposure to the senior people. I came to view operations as a critical role—the fund simply cannot function without it. At times operations can seem like a thankless job, but it can also be a stepping-stone to other parts of the industry. In my experience, most traders are very grateful for your help. It's important to get in good with the traders and analysts, because if you prove to be adding value and building a relationship with them, moves can happen.

Chapter IX

ACCOUNTING

Hedge fund accounting has grown in importance and stature over the past few years, and much of that is due to the overall maturation of the industry and the sophistication and global/multijurisdictional nature of the investments being made. The growth has led to strong demand for accountants to the point where, in some cases, there is a shortage of qualified talent. That makes the current market a great one for candidates. This chapter includes some actual job specifications from recent searches we worked on. We feel that presenting these is an ideal way to show what hedge funds look for when hiring accountants. They also give good descriptions of the responsibilities of the various accounting roles (you will find these toward the middle of the chapter).

The charge to bring in qualified hedge fund accountants is being led by the new generation of hedge funds that have emerged over the past few years. As with the more established funds, these upstarts are faced with a myriad of accounting rules and regulations and no longer want to outsource what has become a vital part of their operations. In addition to wanting to control their own accounting, some funds also believe service levels from outsourcers have not been adequate. The net result has been a new emphasis on building in-house accounting infrastructure, and to achieve that we've seen funds paying more for entry-level accountants and treating them as valued members of their teams. (For a look at the structure of an accounting group at a hedge fund, see Figure 9.1.)

Depending on their size and investment strategy, hedge funds can have various levels of accounting professionals, all of whom report to the chief financial officer (CFO). For example, the accounting group at large funds (more than $1 billion in assets) could have a multilevel infrastructure headed by a controller, with an assistant controller, accounting manager, senior fund accountant, and fund accountant (at some funds this last position may be called a junior accountant). Midsize funds ($500 million to

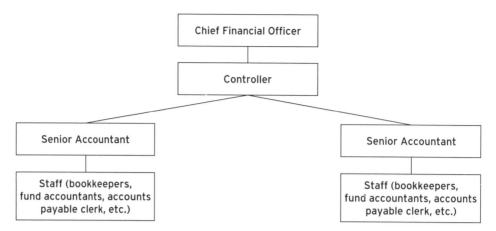

The structure of the accounting group below the chief financial officer level in hedge funds varies depending on the size of the fund. Larger funds could have multiple branches under the chief financial officer with more than one controller. The titles of accountants below the controller level can also vary.

Figure 9.1   Organizational Chart: Accounting

$1 billion) may have one person with an accountant title and a controller reporting to the CFO. Smaller funds might have just one junior person handling the accounting functions. This person could have the title of assistant controller, controller, or senior accountant and would report directly to the CFO. Funds that outsource their accounting functions still need someone to fill an accounting role to work with the fund administrators who handle the accounting.

CAREER PATH

The career path of a hedge fund accountant can be very lucrative, and it's not rare to see CFOs earning packages in the $500,000 range or more. A little lower down the hierarchy, we've seen *guaranteed* offers of $150,000 for assistant controllers—$75,000 base salary and $75,000 bonus. That's not to say that all accountants become CFOs, but there is a definite path that permits junior and senior accountants to grow with their hedge fund and possibly become CFO. Large ($1 billion or more), more established funds would typically bring on accountants with two to five years of experience in the financial services industry to fill junior accountant or fund accountant roles in which they would assist with monthly accounting. At midsize or smaller funds these same individuals can enter as assistant controller or controller and report directly to the CFO. In both cases promotions do happen. From our vantage point, accountants with just one to two years of experience are better off targeting a large fund where they will get basic experience. Having said that, we would also recommend making sure you would be working under a certified public accountant (CPA) who will give you the auditing hours you need to qualify for your own CPA designation.

Regardless of experience, most funds seek candidates who have a four-year degree in accounting and a high GPA. As opposed to front-office positions, hiring firms are less concerned with pedigree when it comes to hiring accountants. Hiring firms put a lot of emphasis on the CPA and want accountants who have passed all parts of the CPA exam. In fact, once an individual has his/her CPA, that becomes the standard more than the school the candidate attended.

As the hedge fund industry has grown in importance, so too has the actual role of accountants. In addition to accounting duties such as profit and loss (P&L) reporting, reconciling internal balances with prime brokers, and monitoring receivables and payables, fund accountants can also be involved in investor relations, risk management, and/or compliance. At smaller firms, senior-level accountants could be put in charge of the fund's operations activities as well.

POSITIONING YOURSELF

One of the major feeders for hedge funds seeking accountants is the Big Four accounting firms. Funds also look at candidates from smaller accounting firms that specialize in financial services or hedge funds. Accountants who have worked with hedge funds as clients and have fund accounting and/or financial services experience are especially desirable. Because of the current shortage of qualified accounting talent at the junior level, hedge funds have also begun to take a look at accountants who lack financial services experience and those who have focused on corporate accounting.

Most funds want to see junior accounting professionals who are not afraid to roll up their sleeves and get into the details of hedge fund accounting. If you are an accountant with the sought-after experience, you can expect recruiters to call you—that is, if you genuinely want to use your accounting skills at a hedge fund (accountants who want to move over to the investment side will find making that switch difficult). Accountants with no financial experience may still get a look from hedge funds, especially if they have a CPA and experience auditing financial services companies.

Hedge funds have a strong need for accountants with product knowledge; thus understanding the securities or instruments that are traded by hedge funds will put you at a distinct advantage. For example, if a hedge fund uses derivatives you should be able to talk about them and know how to put them in whatever trading platform is being used by the hedge fund. One of the best ways to do this is to work in a group that has direct exposure to hedge funds (the investment management group at your accounting firm, a fund administrator, a prime broker, and so on).

Accounting by definition is very detail oriented, and that is paramount when it comes to reconciling trades as they happen. Candidates should have a working knowledge of debits and credits that go into the accounting of securities used in specific hedge fund strategies. To improve your chances of landing a hedge fund accounting position, we recommend you:

- Get as much hedge fund experience as possible. If you haven't worked on hedge fund audits, we suggest doing what you can to get some engagements in financial services.
- Learn the different hedge fund investment strategies. There are accounting differences for each style. For example, whereas a long/short fund will use relatively straightforward accounting, a multistrategy fund will need more detailed accounting.
- Learn as much as you can about the securities in which a specific hedge fund invests.
- Get to know onshore/offshore accounting practices.

Some of the larger funds are showing a need for tax professionals who have worked with K-1 statements. This is a very different role than fund accounting and would typically be suited to people who *only* have tax experience. As a rule of thumb, candidates with tax backgrounds will find it difficult to move into a fund accounting role. If that person truly wants to be on a CFO track, we recommend getting hedge fund accounting experience.

INTERVIEWS

Interviews for accounting positions tend to average three rounds. You will typically begin by meeting the person to whom you would report and one or more of the partners. Unless it is a very large firm, you should expect to meet with most people at the firm. You may be tested on your accounting and product knowledge. Some funds also give a standardized IQ test or a personality test such as the Myers-Briggs Type Indicator. Hedge funds want to hire the best and the brightest, and that intention will extend to noninvestment professionals.

In addition to examining your technical aptitude, your interviewers will scrutinize your personality. In most cases, you would be going from a large institution to a very small firm, and hedge funds will want to see that you can fit into the existing culture of the team. Among other questions, you should expect to be asked:

- Why do you want to work at a hedge fund?
- Why do you want to work at *this* hedge fund?
- What engagements have you been on?
- Have you had exposure to hedge funds?

SAMPLE JOB SEARCHES

To help you better understand the skills sought by hiring firms, take a look at the following actual job specifications.

Search 1: Junior Accountant

Firm that manages long/short equity hedge funds

Responsibilities

- Daily P&L reporting (entering daily trade activity and pricing portfolios for all funds).
- Cash, trade, and position reconciliations (products include equities, futures, swaps, options, and FX).
- Reconciling internal balances with each prime broker.
- Reviewing daily activity on prime broker reports and resolving any differences.
- Assisting with trade clearance and settlement.
- Monitoring receivables and payables.
- Creating and monitoring an additional daily portfolio for accounting and tax issues, including corporation actions, wash sales, and so on.
- Daily entering of trades, corporate actions, and realized and unrealized gains/losses into the portfolio accounting system.

Requirements

- Bachelor's degree in accounting with two to three years of mutual/hedge fund accounting experience (preferably at a hedge fund, hedge fund administrator, or audit firm).
- Knowledge of tax accounting issues, including wash sales, constructive sales, and K-1 preparation.
- Experience with a portfolio accounting system (Advisorware, Advent/Geneva, etc.).
- Detail oriented.
- Ability to multitask and work independently as well as within a small group.
- Proficient with Microsoft Excel.
- Self-motivated and proactive.
- Strong communication and organizational skills.

Search 2: Hedge Fund Accountant

Responsibilities

- Monthly accounting for internally managed hedge funds.
- Assistance in the preparation of monthly, yearly, and life-to-date performance calculations.
- Partnership allocations.
- Consolidation of all accounting entities into monthly board report package.

- Special projects.
- Reading and summarizing legal agreements and external manager correspondence.
- Assisting in the development and implementation of internal controls relative to accounting entities.
- Maintenance of files for proper audit documentation.
- Interactions with other departments, such as trading operations, risk management, and tax.

Requirements

- Bachelor's degree in accounting.
- Computer skills: Excel, Word, Lotus Notes, Bloomberg; Visual Portfolio Manager or other trading software a plus; Platinum or other general ledger packages a plus.
- Two to four years of experience in public accounting (Big Four preferred) and/or private industry with strong background in financial services.
- CPA or on track to get CPA.
- Highly professional demeanor, strong work ethic and initiative, team player.
- Sound written and verbal communication skills.

Search 3: Hedge Fund Assistant Controller

Note: This is a more senior position that would be a number two to the CFO and would assist the CFO/COO with activities of the finance and compliance departments.

Responsibilities

- Assist with month-end fund reconciliation between internal books and administrator's books.
- Create daily performance estimates for investors and fund managers.
- Assist with year-end audits of funds.
- Assist with creation of new funds with prime broker, administrator, and other interested parties.
- Assist with smooth transfer of fund/investor information from finance department to marketing/investor relations department.
- Assist with vendor relationships, billing, and implementation.
- Assist with compliance activities, including:
  - Maintain and review employee brokerage accounts.
  - Assist with monitoring e-mail and other electronic correspondence.
  - Assist with other record-retention policies necessary for investment adviser compliance.
  - Assist with other activities required for a registered investment adviser.
  - Prepare quarterly compliance reports.

Requirements

- Math, accounting, economics, or finance degree from top school.
- One to three years of experience in hedge fund/asset management company or prime brokerage preferred.
- Strong computer skills, specifically in Excel.

Search 4: Controller

This is a more senior position. This firm is seeking someone to report directly to the CFO and managing principals.

Responsibilities

- Monthly partnership accounting/client reports.
- Interface with audit/legal professionals in tax and legal matters.
- Interact with clients.
- Maintain internal systems.
- All other general operations/office management of the firm.

Requirements

- Must have CPA.
- Must have strong finance and operations background and have come directly from a similar role at a fund of funds or hedge fund.
- Must have a combination of business savvy required to interface with senior-level hedge fund professionals and the close attention to detail required to accomplish rigorous job duties accurately and in a timely manner.
- Must have excellent communication skills—both oral and written.
- Must have excellent references.
- Preference for candidates who have experience with Advent Axys and Advent Partner.

CASE STUDY

Case Study 23: An Ideal Accounting Hire

The following case study is an example of someone with a classic accounting background. After studying accounting in undergraduate school, this person went to a Big Four firm where he learned how hedge funds work through his on-site projects. Although he first shied away from an accountant role at a hedge fund, he soon realized that accounting at hedge funds is dramatically different from being an auditor. In addition, he saw that he would gain firsthand insight into all aspects of a fund's activities. As you will read, this person is happy doing what he is doing and has been made to feel like a valued part of the fund's team.

■ ■ ■

I studied accounting with an emphasis on finance and real estate at a West Coast university (class of 2005). Initially I was a business administration major, but the emergence of Sarbanes-Oxley and the demands on corporate reporting led a lot of professors at my school to push students to accounting.

Although I hadn't yet taken an auditing class, I got a summer internship with one of the Big Four accounting firms after my junior year. This position gave me a sense of what auditing was and also of what I wanted to do after graduation. Luckily for me, I got an offer for a full-time position, which allowed me to relax a bit during my senior year. I ended up working in the firm's New York office. This was not a program like the investment banks had where I would be told to move on after two or three years.

I wanted to work in the investment management group so I could learn finance. Just when I began the firm was creating an alternative investment group, and, luckily for me, I was placed into it. Right off the bat I got exposure to hedge funds. In fact, my first on-site audit was with a fund that specialized in mortgage-backed securities. Even though I worked like a dog and didn't have much of a life, I gained a working knowledge of products, including mortgage-backed securities, collateralized debt obligations (CDOs), swaps, repurchase agreements, equities, and bonds. The job also opened my eyes to other opportunities and made me want to work doing investment banking or sales and trading.

I wasn't a big fan of the huge corporate atmosphere of the Big Four firms (they work you to the bone without the bonuses of investment banks), and after a couple of years I began to look at other opportunities. Through a family contact I interviewed at a bulge-bracket bank, but seeing people there work 20 hours a day convinced me that was not for me. I also had a friend who worked on the sales and trading desk of a second-tier firm, but my skills weren't a match. It was then that I decided a middle-office role at a hedge fund or private equity fund would be a good stepping-stone to perhaps work on the investment side.

My desire to work at a hedge fund was solidified by the second accounting project I had—working at a long/short equity fund. Because I was on-site I got to see what the day-to-day life was like at a hedge fund—how the traders and analysts worked and interacted with the controllers and other back-office people. I got along well with the controller and saw that he was involved in many different things at this fund. This type of environment appealed to me. At both of my hedge fund jobs I had extensive interaction with clients, including chief executives, financial officers, and attorneys during all phases of the audit engagement.

I had hopes of getting a front-office position and wasn't sure if I wanted to continue with accounting. I had done some investing on my own and took a value-indexing course in school in which I managed a $100,000 portfolio, so I was not a stranger to the markets and investing. I began working with a recruiter and was sent on an interview with a fund of funds that was looking for an assistant controller. This firm also had a managed account hedge fund and was thinking of getting into private equity as well.

My initial interview was with the head of research and one other person. It was pretty informal. The head of research gave me the background of the firm and its investment philosophy. He also asked me why I was looking to leave my firm and what I was looking to do over the next five years. He wanted to know my skill set and how I could help his firm. Compared to the interview I had at the bulge-bracket firm when I was grilled about swaps and derivatives, this interview didn't get very technical. Maybe that was because I steered the interview and got technical before he could. When he asked what I did at my firm I took the opportunity to be very specific about my role and the accounting I did. I think I explained things in so much detail that there wasn't anything left for him to grill me about. I had a lot to talk about, especially since I had worked those two hedge fund jobs. Without those under my belt I'm sure I wouldn't have gotten the position. In fact, I might not have even gotten the interview.

> *"My advice to any undergrads interested in hedge funds would be to try to pinpoint exactly what they enjoy doing—accounting, selling, investments, marketing, and so on. A lot of young people I meet have a big-picture idea of what they want to do, but seem to have trouble focusing and drilling down to what they really like to do."*

Four months went by without a word from this fund. I was getting busy at my accounting job and working to get my CPA so I didn't get preoccupied with it. Finally, they wanted to see me again and I met with the fund's in-house legal counsel, the CFO, and someone I had met four months earlier. This meeting was arranged hastily and I didn't prepare. I also thought it would be informal like the first interview. I was asked how I would implement internal controls and how I would work with auditors and fund administrators. About a week later I had a third meeting with another of the fund's partners. He started with some technical questions, but it quickly became very conversational. We spoke about music, traveling, and why we enjoy living in New York City. There was nothing to do with accounting or finance. In my gut I had a good feeling about this fund and was eager to get an offer—which I did the following day. This firm has also left open the possibility that if I do well I could move to another area within the fund.

As an assistant controller I am responsible for reviewing and approving fund administration net asset value (NAV) monthly packages (this is part of the process in which we approve monthly capital statements for our investors). I also monitor daily profit and loss in our hedge fund; contact underlying hedge funds for monthly returns for our fund of funds; monitor cash flows available for additional investment (we use multiple bank accounts and banks); deal with auditors, fund administrators, and legal contacts to help produce the financial and capital statements; and deal with tax issues (K-1 statements). I also do midmonth return analysis for large investors and additional analysis and side projects for our CFO.

My advice to any undergrads interested in hedge funds would be to try to pinpoint exactly what they enjoy doing—accounting, selling, investments, marketing, and so on. A lot of young people I meet have a big-picture idea of what they want to do, but seem to have trouble focusing and drilling down to what they really like to do. If someone is an accounting major and wants to remain in accounting, then I'd say going to a Big Four firm would be a good move. While there I'd recommend working in a division that has direct contact with hedge funds as the best way to move to a hedge fund later on. Going straight from undergraduate school to a hedge fund just doesn't happen, so I wouldn't even let it enter your thinking.

If you succeed and get into a hedge fund, you should make sure it is a place where you understand and enjoy the style of investing. In addition you should truly enjoy the people who work there, and that includes the higher-ups. If you don't, then you probably shouldn't be there. In my case, I can honestly say that I really like what I do and could see myself becoming a CFO and liking it.

See Resume L in Appendix B on page 174.

Chapter X

FUND OF HEDGE FUNDS

Fund of hedge funds, or simply fund of funds, have grown into a significant subsector within the hedge fund universe. Because they operate differently from single-manager hedge funds, fund of funds seek to hire professionals with different types of skills than do single-manager funds.

WHAT IS A FUND OF FUNDS?

Rather than investing directly in specific securities, a fund of hedge funds allocates its capital to single-manager hedge funds, which then invest that capital as they would any other investment from a limited partner (LP). As do single-manager funds, fund of funds collect management fees from LPs. Some also charge an incentive fee based on profits. In either case, both fees would be in addition to those charged by the underlying funds, creating a double layer of fees for the investor.

There are two main categories of fund of funds: diversified, in which assets are invested in various types of hedge funds, and niche, which invest in hedge funds with the same investment strategy. Since fund of funds invest in a selection of different funds with different asset classes, they tend to provide a more stable long-term investment return than any of the individual funds.

A MAJOR ASSET CLASS

Fund of funds have grown considerably over the past few years to the point where they currently account for a significant portion of the overall hedge fund market. In fact, as of the end of the first quarter of 2007 fund of hedge fund assets under management (AUM) totaled $1.14 trillion, representing about 48% of the global industry, according to HedgeFund.net. As the market has grown, so too have fund sizes.

By the end of 2006, the average size of a fund of hedge funds had reached $178 million, from $21 million in 2001, according to the *2007 Eureka Global Fund of Hedge Funds Directory*. The Eureka survey also found that:

- More than half (55%) of all fund of hedge funds have less than $100 million in AUM.
- Fully 29% of all fund of hedge funds are based in the United States, and 24% are in the United Kingdom. Switzerland (17%), various offshore financial centers (14%), and France (5%) are the other leading domiciles for fund of funds.
- Long/short equity funds account for one-third of the total, followed by multi-strategy funds with 20%.
- Emerging markets–focused funds are attracting the most new assets and have produced the best returns over the past five years.
- About 60% of Asian fund of hedge funds are managed out of the United States and UK.
- Over the past few years, fund of funds with more than $1 billion in assets have performed consistently better than their smaller peers.
- Fees account for 22.5% of fund of funds returns, in contrast to absolute return funds, where fees represent less than 7% of the total.

ROLES AND RESPONSIBILITIES

Working at a fund of hedge funds is very different than at a single-manager fund, and therefore the types of candidates sought by fund of funds are also distinct. At a fund of funds, analysts are not involved in direct investments; they focus most of their time on researching and monitoring managers of the hedge funds in which the fund of funds allocates capital. They focus on the managers' backgrounds, reputations, and the types of investments they make, as well as a host of quantitative analyses such as risk-adjusted returns and volatility. In addition to helping select the fund managers, analysts at fund of funds keep tabs on the performance of the underlying funds and decide whether to stay with each manager or switch their allocation in favor of another.

Anyone looking to break into a fund of hedge funds for the first time would most likely be brought on as an analyst (sometimes called junior analyst) to support the senior analysts. They are part of the team that conducts managerial due diligence on the underlying hedge funds, but they are not making allocation decisions. That is the role of the investment committee or portfolio manager. When conducting research, analysts visit the hedge fund managers and look at both qualitative factors—what the hedge fund invests in, the portfolio manager's reputation, what the investment strategy is, what risk controls are in place, and what manager turnover is like at the fund—and quantitative factors—the fund's performance, redemptions, asset growth, and volatility. (For an organizational chart of a typical large fund of funds, see Figure 10.1.)

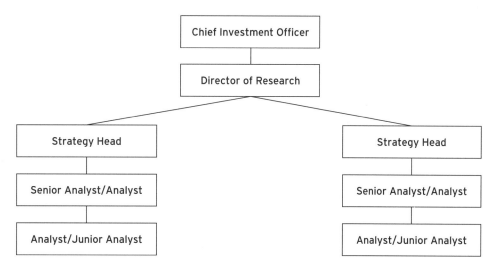

Figure 10.1   Organizational Chart: Fund of Funds

Firms looking to hire at this level typically seek individuals with one to three years of experience. While most funds hire out of the investment banking and consulting programs, some of the larger, more established funds that may bring on a few people each year may also recruit at the undergraduate level. Those firms that are comfortable hiring at the undergrad level will target individuals from top schools with knowledge of finance, business, or accounting and who have strong Excel skills. When hiring bankers or consultants, fund of funds do not compete for the same talent that is typically sought by hedge funds. They also have more flexibility when it comes to the groups at investment banks from which they hire. Another pool of candidates for a fund of funds is investment consultants and private wealth advisers, as they do similar due diligence on money managers. Having an MBA is not a prerequisite to getting a position at a fund of funds. If you do have one, however, you would come in at a slightly higher level than those without. Fund of funds have also been known to hire junior buy-side analysts.

After joining as an analyst/junior analyst, the typical career path is to move up to a senior analyst position and then to a strategy head/CIO/director of research. Those titles usually serve on the fund's investment committee and are the ones making allocation decisions. At the senior analyst level, fund of funds look for people with direct due diligence experience, meaning they are usually hired from other fund of funds.

Glocap Insight

If your true dream is to pick stocks and make investment decisions, you should not try to convince a fund of funds that working there is your true life's calling.

While someone can certainly switch from a single-manager fund to a fund of funds, it is rare to make the opposite move.

No matter who they are hiring, fund of funds are always concerned that candidates know their role will be different than it would be at a single-manager fund. In terms of specific skills, hiring firms will want to see that you have a general interest in the public markets and that you follow them. While having invested on your own would be helpful, it is not a prerequisite to working at a fund of funds. As we noted, fund of funds select managers, not individual stocks, so they want people who can take a more macro view of the markets. Writing is also an essential tool, as analysts are constantly putting together reports on the manager they are researching.

Although compensation at a fund of funds is generally less than what it is for successful investment professionals at single-manager funds, the work can be more relaxed and the lifestyle less stressful—two advantages that are usually emphasized by hiring firms. Positions at fund of funds also tend to be more stable. And while fund of funds analysts are not researching individual stocks and making investment recommendations, they can control where a fund's money is invested and can therefore wield considerable power. Working at a fund of hedge funds may not be a stepping-stone to a position at a single-manager hedge fund, but it will provide exposure to a wide range of hedge funds and investment styles. You would see firsthand how hedge funds make money.

Interviews at fund of funds tend to be more focused on personality/fit and macro-level issues and market trends. They will also expect you to have a good understanding of the different hedge fund investing styles.

SAMPLE JOB SEARCHES

Here are some specifications from actual job searches we worked on. Reading these should help emphasize what fund of hedge funds look for when hiring.

Search 1: Junior Analyst

This multibillion-dollar fund of hedge funds is seeking a junior analyst to join its manager selection team. The firm prefers a recent college graduate or a candidate with one year of experience in a financial field.

Responsibilities

- The analyst's primary role will be to support the firm's investment professionals with various investment research and related tasks and projects.
- The analyst's duties may also include managing and updating the firm's investment database, spreadsheets, and related files.

- The analyst will be expected to attend industry conferences and seminars, and to participate in various research, portfolio management, and risk management activities and meetings, all as appropriate.

Requirements

- Up to three years of capital markets/investment management experience.
- Strong desire to work in the investment management industry.
- Solid academic record in a quantitatively challenging discipline/program.
- High level of proficiency with Microsoft Excel and Access programs.
- Strong written and oral communication skills.

Search 2: Analyst

This $2 billion fund is seeking a research analyst to support its senior analysts on the due diligence team.

Responsibilities

- Conduct analyses and run models in support of the senior analysts' due diligence meetings.
- Assist in the production of research reports.
- Assist in the due diligence and monitoring of investment managers.

Requirements

- Must have one to two years of experience in the financial services industry; asset management and/or investment banking backgrounds a plus.
- Must have superior Excel skills, with the ability to build macros and pivot tables; knowledge of VBA a plus.
- Must be organized, detail-oriented, and able to prioritize multiple projects.
- Must be a highly motivated team player.

CASE STUDY

Case Study 24: A Typical Fund of Funds Hire

This person had the ideal background for a fund of funds. As a consultant he worked at a firm that specialized in asset management and he had direct exposure to hedge funds. In essence he was doing a lot of the same due diligence work as is performed by a fund of funds.

Knowing he lacked the background for an investment position, he targeted fund of funds and realized his goal.

■ ■ ■

For someone who ended up in finance, I definitely had a less traditional background. And, while others knew early on that they wanted finance, my interest didn't take shape until I had finished school. I graduated from an Ivy League college in 2003 with a degree in business administration and was thinking of a career in the hospitality industry, perhaps in a restaurant or hotel. After graduation I spent two and a half months traveling in Europe.

My life-altering moment came when I was staying with a cousin who runs a hedge fund in Europe. I ended up not only staying with him, but shadowing him to work for a month. It became a type of unpaid internship during which time I watched how he traded. I also went on, and listened to, client and investment calls with him. By sitting at the trading desk and observing the fund's senior currency trader, I learned the basic principles of momentum trading as well as the overall principles of foreign exchange and futures trading. The fund was small enough—five investment professionals and a small operations staff—that I basically learned how the entire operation functioned. My experience at this fund convinced me that I wanted to learn more about, and possibly work in, the asset management industry.

When I returned to the United States I began to interview. I had a lot of friends in banking programs, but since I hadn't done a junior year internship, I didn't think I could get into one and hadn't pursued that route while I was at school. Fortunately, a friend from college who had graduated one year ahead of me called and told me that the consulting firm where he was working was interviewing. This firm has a large practice advising asset managers (hedge funds among them), and I knew I would be exposed to a lot of different firms and see how they operate, how their workers interact, and how they make investment decisions. I thought it would be a great way to learn about, and then help me get into, the buy side. I also knew I would learn a lot about hedge funds and would meet many people at those funds.

During my three years at this firm I worked with about 45 different asset management firms, about 10 of which were hedge funds or fund of funds. In addition, I analyzed over 40 long-only and alternative managers on performance quality, investment process, distribution best practices, and investment skill. I also conducted market trend research on equity, fixed income, and alternative investments. Many of my projects were on-site so I got a firsthand view of how these firms worked.

After three years I felt I was ready to move on. Although I interviewed at some private equity and single-manager hedge funds, I knew that my skill set and background made me better suited for a fund of hedge funds (I didn't have the banking and/or private equity background that is pretty much a requirement to work at a single-manager fund). I was aware that analysts at fund of funds spend a great deal of time analyzing and evaluating the investment capabilities and operational skill and competency of hedge fund managers—just what I had been doing as a consultant. In addition to having met, and interacted with, many hedge fund managers, I felt that being young and moldable would also make me appealing to a fund of funds. I had also worked with a large private equity fund that had purchased a fund of hedge funds and helped write a white paper on institutional investors' involvement in hedge funds, so I was familiar with the overall industry.

I went through three rounds of interviews at the fund from which I ended up getting an offer. This firm was big enough that I was confident it was here to stay, but also small enough to allow room for growth. That was important to me, as I wanted a place where I could be with senior people who would take the time to mentor and teach me. My first interview was with the two senior research analysts who were the co-heads of the firm's investment committee. These two people kind of played the good-cop, bad-cop routine. One wanted to hear about my background and my career path to date. He asked why I wanted to work at this particular fund. The second executive grilled me about my knowledge of the hedge fund industry. He wanted me to tell him about a manager I had met and why I liked or didn't like that manager. He wanted to hear about a project I had worked on and the research I had done and then probed my feelings about the industry some more. I was confident about my knowledge of the hedge fund industry and had no problem giving my opinion about the role of pension funds and how I thought there would be increased regulatory scrutiny. It became an intellectual conversation about the state of the industry, and I wasn't afraid to disagree with him, as long as I had valid reasons to back up my ideas. I remember being asked if I thought fund of funds would still be around in 10 years and being able to cite the reasons why I was sure they would be.

"Hedge funds are in the news all the time and are very sexy, but if you come in for the wrong reasons anyone in the business will see right through you."

After about one week I was called back for a second round of interviews. This time I met with the COO and was asked more personality/fit questions. He also wanted to know what I thought about the hedge fund industry and what I expected from the job. I then met the rest of the analyst team—four other analysts—as a group. These were the people with whom I would be working. I was asked some of the same questions as before, and also why I was looking to move into hedge funds. I made sure to have some questions for them, so I asked them to walk me through a typical day. I also wanted to know where they needed help so I could see where I would fit into the group.

My final interview was with the CEO of the firm. It was scheduled to last 40 minutes but went on for two hours. This person is not known for wasting his time, so I took it as a good sign that he wanted to talk with me for so long. He got a little more specific than I thought he would, asking me questions such as how did I think high net worth individuals should be invested. I got a written offer soon thereafter and accepted.

I would advise any person interested in working at a hedge fund (single-manager or fund of funds) to question their reasons. Hedge funds are in the news all the time and are very sexy, but if you come in for the wrong reasons anyone in the business will see right through you. Yes, you can do very well financially and there are some 25-year-olds who get huge bonuses, but you cannot go in saying that is why you want to work there. You will be questioned as to why you want hedge funds, so you need a long-term plan. You will gain the respect of anyone who meets you if you can point out that you had a plan when you graduated from college and show how you took steps to make that plan work out. (It's extremely rare that someone goes directly from college to a hedge fund—unless they have a contact, and that is a bit like cheating.) Having invested on your own since you were 16 may be a compelling story, but if that doesn't describe you, then you will have to find something that makes you compelling.

In general, I think it is important to make it clear to people interviewing you that the job at their firm is on your career track and that your old job is not. You should explain that you are leaving your old job because it isn't getting you where you want to be in five years. If an interviewer thinks you are moving into hedge funds for money or because you had problems at your old job, you are going to get nixed early in the interview process. However, if you explain how your old job was a great learning experience and got you into a position where you could go after the job you really wanted, then that is compelling.

I'd also recommend that anyone interested in fund of funds go after professional credentials such as the Chartered Financial Analyst (CFA) or Chartered Alternative Investment Analyst (CAIA). Working in a fund of funds takes strong quantitative and great communication skills, and it's hard to find people with that mix of skills. If someone has those credentials under their belt it will show that they are committed to the space.

Chapter XI

THE RESUME

In our view, the main goal of a resume is to get you considered by a recruiter or a hiring firm—in this case, a hedge fund. To that end, this chapter outlines some of our suggestions about what should be included and how the resume should appear. In Appendix B you will find 12 resumes that correspond to some of the case studies that appeared throughout the earlier chapters of this book. Each of the resumes has our "Recruiter's Perspectives" at the top highlighting what we believe makes the candidate stand out.

Before submitting a resume, you should know that recruiters, and for that matter almost anyone in a hiring position, are very adept at judging the merits of a candidate after a quick scan of a resume. The format, the words, and even the font you use can be indicators of who you are and can play a role in either getting a recruiter or a hiring firm excited or turning them off.

In our opinion, when putting together a resume your goal should be to present an accurate and complete picture of yourself and what you have done, with the hope of getting an interview (when you will present yourself and your qualifications in person). Think of your resume as your calling card—your one shot to be seen by a recruiter or hiring firm. It must be clean and neat. On the flip side, you should, at all costs, strive to avoid harming yourself by putting together a document that is too busy to be easily readable or one that uses excessive (and unnecessary) embellishment or over-the-top phrases (see "The Personal Section" later in the chapter). Remember, the main goal of the resume is to get in the door. We want you to maximize your experiences on paper, and we don't want you to miss out on an interview because you left something off of your resume or because you worded it wrong. With that in mind, here are some general suggestions on what we think you should and should not include and how best to organize your resume.

127

FORMAT

Overall, we look for crisp and clean resumes presented in an easy-to-read format (try using margins that are flush right and left) that use simple fonts and have zero typographical errors. Even one typo, one off-colored font or format, or an uncalled-for item in a personal section could be enough to separate one qualified candidate from another (remember, typos aren't always picked up by spell-checkers, so always read your resume thoroughly before sending it in). We should be able to look at your resume and quickly see where you work (and in which department if that is important), what you do, where you went to school, and at least one personal thing that makes you stand out.

We tend to like resumes with as little white space as possible, but also don't want to see too much information crammed onto the page. We also prefer separating job responsibilities and achievements with bullet points rather than dashes or using long sentences. We don't want to see a novel—and neither do the hiring firms.

THE OBJECTIVE

In our opinion, the only time an objective is necessary at the beginning of a resume is when someone is making a major career transition. Otherwise, your resume should make it obvious what position you are looking for.

KEEP IT TO ONE PAGE

For us, a resume is always one page, especially for anyone with 10 years or less of work experience. We have seen very senior people squeeze their experiences onto one page, so you should be able to as well. The exception to this rule is if you have specific additional information—such as a deal sheet, a list of patents you were granted, or papers you have published. These can be included as part of a supplemental appendix.

BE HONEST

You are who you are, and your resume is not a place to change anything. That means don't list things you have not done or embellish things that you have. Expect that your resume will be checked, and this includes test scores, GPAs, work experiences, and athletic accomplishments (some firms ask for transcripts or graduation degrees, and almost all ask for references and will check them). Putting in something that doesn't belong is simply not worth the risk. Also, never leave off any part of your full-time work history, however short it may be.

JOBS: BE AS DESCRIPTIVE AS POSSIBLE

Hedge funds want to see what you have done. For bankers, that means listing your deals. You should break all deals down individually and list your responsibilities along with the size of the deal, the structure used, and the status, such as whether the deal has closed or is pending. Consultants should do the same for projects. If you are coming from an equity research background, you should list your area of coverage and what your specific responsibilities were. If you were ranked by any trade publications (for example, *Institutional Investor*), those should be mentioned as well as any significant recommendation you made. Traders should mention the sectors and specific products they trade—if stocks, list the names. If you account for P&L, mention that. If you have a relationship with the buy side, listing your major accounts may help. In either case, don't list what you are not prepared to talk about.

HAVE YOU INVESTED?

Any investing experience must be clearly listed. This is precisely what hedge funds want to see, and they will ask you about it. Were you in an investment club in school? Did you participate in a stock selection competition? If you've invested on your own, a simple line in the personal section that reads "Actively follow markets" may be enough. Anything more detailed could pique the interest of a hedge fund, though.

ANYTHING IS FAIR GAME

Whether it's a deal you worked on, a class you attended, or a trip you took, you should be prepared to talk about everything on your resume, and this includes things that you list as hobbies or personal interests. If you say you speak conversational German, there is a chance your interviewer is fluent and may ask you something in German. If you think you will stumble with that, then don't list it. Your resume is what you want people to know about you, so make sure you have an answer to everything that is listed.

DON'T FORGET THE MONTHS

Although some well-known guidelines suggest otherwise, we think it's beneficial to try to always list the month and year you started and ended a position. If you left a job in December 2007 but your resume just says "2007," someone reading your resume in January 2008 will not know if you have been out of work for 10 days, 10 weeks, or 10 months.

MIND THE GAPS

While it's perfectly understandable if someone has a gap in their employment history, it must be explained. If you were between jobs and worked as a consultant or stayed at home to take care of a newborn, you must say so. If you are currently employed, your first job listing should say "2006–Present." Likewise, if you are not employed, your resume should have an accurate representation of when you left your last job and not imply that you are still working.

TEST SCORES MATTER

Undergraduate GPAs are relevant for nearly your entire career. Always list them to at least one decimal point. Some people with high GPAs sell themselves short by not including them because they "heard it does not matter once you are more senior or post B-school." List GMAT and SAT scores, especially if they are good to great. (We would recommend holding off if they are very low.) For MBAs, business school GPAs are not worth including, but top class distinctions are, such as a Baker Scholar from Harvard Business School or an Arjay Miller Scholar from the Stanford Graduate School of Business.

WHAT ABOUT HIGH SCHOOL?

High school information should generally not be included unless it is significant— for example, valedictorian of 500-student graduating class or class president. Some graduates of prep or private schools may list the schools, as those ties among alumni could be pretty strong. Listing an accomplishment such as being captain of a varsity team, member of an honor society, or member of a championship team are acceptable, but the listing should be brief.

THE PERSONAL SECTION

Always include a personal section on your resume. This is the one and only area where you can be creative. List some hobbies/interests/accomplishments that are truly your own. Do not try to write ones that you think people are going to want to read—avid crocodile wrestler, drag racer, or base jumper—unless you really do those things. Firms and recruiters can see through that and size you up pretty quickly. Golf, hiking, fly-fishing, coaching soccer, playing piano, tutoring, photography, ballroom dancing, judo, and traveling are all pretty descriptive and neutral. Being a contestant on college Jeopardy or having been a child actor are also interesting if you want to include them. Wine tasting, reading spy novels, driving the Amalfi Coast, and being an avid Cincinnati Reds fan are all acceptable but approaching the limits. Smoking fine cigars while drinking single malt whiskey, playing with my two *beautiful* children, intellectual political commentary, and watching ESPN are probably over the top and could potentially hurt you.

LANGUAGE/INTERNATIONAL

Language skills may be included in your personal section. However, if you are pushing for an international career you could list them separately, adding levels of proficiency (e.g., native French speaker, fluent in Spanish and business Spanish, conversational in Mandarin). The same goes for dual citizenship, which can work to your advantage if you want an overseas job and could be in your personal section or a separate area.

SOME OTHER DOs AND DON'Ts

- Deemphasize older, less relevant work experience (e.g., summer jobs unless brand-name firms or jobs during college).
- There is never a need to write "References available upon request." However, you had better have references and be prepared for them to be checked.
- In the current world of e-mail, don't worry about paper. In most cases if a resume needs to be printed it will be the recruiter printing it and sending it on to a client, so sending in a resume on fancy paper stock is not necessary.
- Whatever contact information you include is fair game, so make sure what you list (e-mail, mobile phone, work phone, home phone) is in working order and that it is okay for a recruiter or firm to use.

In Appendix B are 12 resumes that correspond to some of the case studies throughout the earlier part of this guide. We have altered these to protect the identities of the people who were gracious enough to allow us to reprint them. In some cases the resumes may seem short. That is because they only reflect each person's work experiences leading up to his or her first hedge fund position. Rather than advocating the style and format of these resumes, we present them as they are to show the academic and career progressions that made them attractive to hedge funds.

We recommend you look at all of the resumes in Appendix B—those of people with the ideal experience and even those without it—but we suggest you make an extra effort to look for a resume from someone who is at the same entry point as you and compare your background to theirs. Also, take a look at what makes each person stand out and how they conveyed that in their resume; sometimes it's their personal experiences, while other times it's their academic or professional accomplishments.

When you look at the resumes, focus on how they describe their work experiences and what they include in the personal sections. To help you out, each resume has a section at the top called "Recruiter's Perspective" in which we point out the strong points and the items that jump out at recruiters and hiring firms when scanning the resume. Some resumes also have some notes under "Pluses." These are not the ubiquitous action words that many resume guides suggest using; rather they are specific achievements that give the candidate special points in the eyes of a recruiter. Without these pluses the candidate would likely still be a strong candidate, but with them he or she has something extra that moves up a notch, at least in the opinion of our recruiters. Rankings of undergraduate institutions on each resume come from *U.S. News & World Report*'s list of America's Best Colleges 2007. The business school rankings are from *BusinessWeek*'s 2006 ranking of the best MBA programs (this ranking is done every two years).

Chapter XII

THE INTERVIEW

Getting an interview at a hedge fund is just the first part of securing a job. *Impressing* your interviewers and *convincing* them that they should hire you over the scores of other people they may meet should be your goal.

Before we begin, we should point out that if you are working with a recruiter you will almost certainly be asked many of the same questions listed in this chapter before being sent on a formal interview. In that case, we suggest preparing for your recruiter interviews as much as you would for your job interviews.

In addition to our advice in this chapter, we suggest you read (or reread) the case studies that appear throughout the preceding chapters, as they contain additional insight into the interview process. They also mention specific questions that candidates were asked (some of which we review in this chapter).

THE PROCESS

Interviews for investment professionals at most hedge funds are about four rounds. Although the actual questions can vary from one fund to another, for investment professional roles, most want to see that a candidate is truly passionate about the public markets and investing. The funds want candidates who know finance and accounting and truly enjoy investing. At the end of the day, hedge funds are focused on who they think is smart and on making sure there is a cultural fit. To that end, the early rounds will include a mix of qualitative (personality/fit) and quantitative (more technical) questions. If you get a take-home case study or are asked to prepare a presentation, this will take place in a later round. You may have to present the idea to the entire hedge fund team. Here is what a typical analyst recruiting process could look like at a long/short fund:

- **Round 1:** Candidates will likely meet with one or two people who will gauge the candidate's personality, business judgment, and financial skills. At some funds candidates may meet more than one person and may even meet some noninvestment professionals, though that usually occurs more toward the later rounds.
- **Round 2:** If the candidate is deemed a fit, there will be meetings with more people at the fund. The second round could include a written exam that may test overall market awareness, finance and accounting skills, and logic. Some funds may also give personality or IQ tests.
- **Round 3:** You may be asked to present an idea to the fund's investment committee.
- **Round 4:** This is typically a more informal round that could be a dinner with one of the senior members of the fund or another type of relaxed meeting. If you've gotten this far, you will more than likely be presented with a verbal offer.

No matter where you interview, expect the process to be extensive. That point was underscored by the author of Case Study 3:

> The whole interview process can be pretty overwhelming, grueling, and frustrating. At almost every interview I had I was forced to think in new ways that were completely alien to me. Although this was frustrating, I realized that being a professional investor forces one to continuously think in novel ways, and in order to succeed in an environment like that one has to be flexible and innovative in one's thought process. Until I realized this and was comfortable with it, the interview process seemed like it was going to last forever.

It doesn't matter if you're interviewing at a large or a small fund, a long/short or a global macro one; all hedge funds want people who can add value to their bottom line, and therefore a lot of the questions and tests will focus on determining whether you can help the fund make money. The author of Case Study 2 describes his interviews:

> The first rounds of most interviews were usually pretty informal, with some finance questions mixed in (if you were required to bring a stock pick or take a test, they usually informed you ahead of time so you could prepare). I was always asked why I was interested in hedge funds and why I wanted to work at the particular fund where I was being interviewed. Sometimes first-round interviews can get a little more complex. During the first round at one fund I was given two investment options; one had an IRR (internal rate of return) of 20% and the other had an IRR of 30%. I was asked if there was any reason not to invest in the one with the higher IRR. In this case, the fund wanted me to understand what IRR meant at a deeper level and to know that a lot depends on how much you can invest and how long you can keep it invested. I was often asked what my weaknesses were (and each time was told not to say that I work too hard).

> **Insider Tip** ▷
>
> **Senior Hedge Fund Executive**
> "When my firm recently hired a junior person, we began with 300 resumes. We whittled the list down to about 35, then used phone screens to pare it down to 15, whom we then met face-to-face. I've got to admit I ran a pretty anal process, but that's because I had so many people to choose from. I used the phone interviews to test people's ability to communicate concisely. In this business there is no time for rambling answers, even when people are talking about themselves. If you can't answer the 'Tell me about yourself' question in 25 seconds, then you've lost me. Then I would throw a math question at them—something like, 'What is eight basis points times 14 million?' That type of question lets me see if they know what a basis point is, can multiply 8×14 quickly, and not get flustered. If their answer is off by a factor of 10 I still give them credit, but if their answer begins with anything other than 112 then they're off."

At the MBA level, many funds have one long initial day of interviews that could last about six hours. It's possible that you may not hear back from them for a month while they meet other people. One MBA candidate noted that hedge funds don't interview people at the same time, and not getting in touch with you is their way of seeing how you follow up after your initial interview. It goes back to the type of person they are looking for. They want to hire the person who, when analyzing a potential investment, will be the one to make the extra call that unearths a crucial piece of information.

SOME GENERAL TIPS

There are some basic steps that you can take to prepare for interviews at all hedge funds—and for that matter with a recruiter. Focusing on only these will not guarantee smooth sailing, but ignoring them could hurt your chances of advancing. With that in mind, here are a few points that everyone should know:

• Know your resume cold. You should be able to walk someone through your resume—typically starting with your undergraduate experience. Know and be able to communicate the rationales for all of your decisions. As the person in Case Study 12 put it:

> In terms of interviewing, I'd say you should practice enough so your answers become second nature. Don't BS your interviewers. Make sure you can speak to everything on your resume, and don't list deals that you can't speak about for at least 30 minutes. You don't want to look like an idiot. You should be able to spin any experience that you've had into something that would apply to the job you're interviewing for.

- If you are coming from a banking background, it's essential to know your deals (often a probing question). This includes being able to speak intelligently about your responsibilities on the deal (for example, origination, modeling, due diligence, negotiations, interaction with management team, travel, operational/strategic work). You should know all numbers involved in the deal and understand the big picture: why the deal was beneficial or not (value drivers). Would you invest in the deal if you were allowed to?

- Know as much as possible about the firms at which you interview, including their investment styles and backgrounds of professionals, assets under management, number of investment professionals, fund performance, actual investments, and investor base. Note the advice outlined in Case Study 2:

  > Overall, there is very little standardization among questions asked during hedge fund interviews. I've been asked everything under the sun. I'd say it's important to know the various hedge fund styles and which suits your background. If you go into an interview and are not interested/knowledgeable in what the fund invests in, your interviewer will see it and pick up on it, meaning if you're interested in equities and find yourself interviewing at a fund that specializes in debt, your interviewer will pick up on your ambivalence/lack of knowledge about the fund.

- Funds will want to know why you are interested in working at their specific fund, so come prepared with questions that demonstrate your interest in what the fund does. The person in Case Study 4 had the right attitude:

  > I used this round of interviews to ask questions about the firm—just like a good investor will have questions for a company, I had a list of questions to ask my interviewers, and they liked my curiosity. Before going on my first interview, I Googled risk arbitrage/event-driven hedge funds and learned as much as I could. When they asked me if I knew what the style was I was able to give the short, textbook answer, and I was able to tell them that I wanted to learn more about it.

- Keep up with current events. This includes the hedge fund market as well as the broader market. When talking about the markets, it's important to have a specific view. It doesn't matter if you are right or wrong as long as you have reasons for your ideas.

Insider Tip ▷

Hedge Fund Executive
"If I'm hiring someone for a junior position it is important that the person not come off like a know-it-all. The candidates need to be junior enough to roll up their sleeves and follow my every command."

- Know the roles and responsibilities of the role for which you are interviewing (it can differ from fund to fund).

- Don't discount the importance of fit. Most hedge funds are small (in terms of the number of professionals) and can be a pressure-cooker environment because they are dealing with the public markets. Hedge funds are marked to market daily, so if you make a pick and it goes wrong you will know pretty fast. It takes a specific type of personality to work in such an environment, and your interviewers will spend a lot of time trying to get to know you and see if you are someone who can fit in with the team already in place.

THE "WHY HEDGE FUND?" QUESTION

Without a doubt you will be asked, "Why are you interested in hedge funds?" With more and more people wanting to work in hedge funds, it's important that you want to work for the right reasons—that you are curious about the public markets and have a passion for investing—and that you can state them in a convincing manner.

Insider Tip ▷

Senior Analyst
"You always want to be as prepared and effusive as possible for an interview. What impresses people most is when you can answer questions and when it's clearly apparent that you believe those answers yourself."

INVESTING

Unless you are interviewing at a quantitative type fund, you will be asked if you invest on your own or have done so in the past. Your interviewers will want to hear specifics about your past investments and what your thought processes were. It may not matter if you talk about your most or least successful investment, your latest purchase or your very first one; what is important is your ability to explain why you invested and your reasons for making the investment. The facts, figures, and reasons should roll off your tongue as naturally as possible. Those include what you bought, when you bought it, and at what price, but can get more detailed depending on your answers. If you can rattle off the date you purchased something, the price, and the reason, you will be in good shape. For example, "I invested in Banana Republic. I bought 500 shares at $X on January 1, 2002, because [give convincing reason]. I sold the shares 10 months later at $X." Take another look at how the person in Case Study 3 described the questions he was asked:

> In all my interviews I was asked if I invested and what the *motivation* behind my investments was. Was I putting money to work just because I had too much in savings or because my dad had told me to put some money in a mutual fund? Were there other reasons? Of course, they wanted to hear that I was truly interested in the markets and

finding undervalued companies. . . . Once I answered the "Do you invest?" question positively, my interviewers would typically jump right in and bombard me with questions about my analysis and the specifics of each investment. What do you invest in? Why did you buy that stock? Where is it trading? At what price did you buy it? What do the horizons look like for the next five years? What is your price target?

If you have not invested on your own before (no money, repaying student loans, compliance restrictions from your investment bank, or some other reason), you should at least be able to walk through an investment you *would* make if you had the time and/or money. You should also be ready to discuss the current state of the market. The goal is to come across as a potential investor regardless of any limitations you may have. It wouldn't help your cause to say, "I've been working 100 hours a week and haven't had the time to invest." If you haven't invested before, it's better to admit that. In that case it's even more imperative that you start thinking about investing.

PERSONAL/FIT QUESTIONS

Anything is fair game when it comes to personal questions. Remember, most hedge funds are smaller than investment banks and consulting firms. The people sit next to and work with each other for long hours. Your interviewers will want to get a sense of who you are and what it will be like to work with you. The author of Case Study 4 summed up this part of the interview process:

> You can't get around the fact that if the people at a fund don't like you they won't hire you. In addition to judging whether they liked me, I think the people I met were trying to determine if I could learn their style of investing.

The individual in Case Study 1 adds:

> During the first 20 minutes at the hedge fund, my interviewer, a partner with whom I now work closely, focused on getting to know me and I was not asked a single finance question. Rather, he asked things like: What school did you go to? Did you like it? What activities did you do there? Did you like your investment bank? Why are you leaving? (It would not be a good idea to answer that by saying you didn't like working 100 hours a week or because you wanted to make more money.) Are you a social person? What do you do on the weekends? Like many other interviewers, he asked me about some of my more interesting hobbies and things that we had in common (for instance, we both really like hockey).

Other candidates told us they were asked questions such as:

- Would you tell us about yourself?
- Do you like working in a collaborative environment?
- What's your favorite movie?
- What music do you like?

- Where did you grow up?
- What do your parents do? How do you think that affected your personality?
- What do you do in your free time?
- Why did you choose the college you went to?

Insider Tip ▷

Senior Analyst

"Fit is a huge aspect, not only in terms of a person's interpersonal fit, but also in their willingness to embrace a new process. I've had people walk in and think, 'I'm the man and I know how to do things.' That may work in some funds, but not in ours."

TECHNICAL QUESTIONS

As with personality questions, the technical- or finance-related questions can be as varied as the different hedge fund styles. All funds will expect that you have solid knowledge of finance and accounting and may test your ability to read financial statements and construct financial models. It's best to be ready for anything and prepare for everything. In Case Study 3, the author points out:

> They asked me to walk them through an LBO and dissect a company's financial statements. They asked my opinion of a company I had never heard of before. I knew they wanted to find out how I thought and formulated my investment ideas. I'd say 90% of the hedge funds out there are looking to see how people analyze problems and show they can approach a situation from both a micro and macro level.

BRAINTEASERS/LOGIC QUESTIONS/PROBLEMS

Hedge funds are known for asking brainteasers/logic and problem-solving questions. As these are designed more to see how you analyze and tackle the problem than to score you on the actual answer, there may be no effective way to prepare for them. Here's a sampling of some brainteasers and problems (several of them were mentioned in the case studies):

- What is the formula of Poisson distribution?
- If you have infinite volatility in an option, what would the graph look like?
- What degrees are in the hour and minute hands of a clock if it is 3:30?
- Count by powers of 2.
- Here's company X. A well-known investor is proposing to buy company X and merge it with one of his other holdings. Take a look at the stock price, and, using the financials, give your view on company X's valuation.

- You have companies A and B. One has a higher EBITDA and the other has a more levered balance sheet. Which situation would you rather have?
- You've been given two hours to examine the financials of a company. If you own every part of its capital structure, what would you do with the different securities of the company and the company itself?

THOUGHT-PROVOKING QUESTIONS

Some funds may ask more questions designed to see how you think.

- In your daily life, where do you find value?
- Why did you write what you wrote for your senior thesis?
- How do you define whether something is expensive?
- Why should we hire you?
- What book did you like best in your life and why?
- On a scale of A to F, how would you grade yourself on this interview?
- What are your life goals?
- What was the best advice you were ever given?

INVESTMENT IDEAS/CASE STUDIES

If you are interviewing for an investment professional position, you will be asked for an investment idea. For example, if you're interviewing at a long/short fund you may be asked for a short and a long idea. Be prepared with at least one investment idea. Make sure the idea is appropriate for the type of firm at which you are interviewing. Some firms will ask you to come back with a lengthy presentation, while others may ask for one on the spot. If you get this far in the process, your performance on these presentations will go a long way toward determining whether you get an offer. Your interviewers are looking to see how you judge value and present your ideas. The author of Case Study 1 outlines what he did when asked for an investment idea:

> You must be prepared with a view. The people interviewing you want to see your thoughts and logic. They may challenge your assumptions, so it's important to keep your cool. And, if they point out something to you that you didn't know, it's okay to say something like "I never thought of it that way," but try to make this new idea align with your overall viewpoint. I always had one trading idea ready that I knew inside and out and also two backups that I could speak about. For the first I could rattle off historical revenue and EBITDA figures for three years and my investment's macroeconomic drivers. I knew what was going on in my company, its industry and competitors, and any major changes that had occurred in the past couple of years. I could speak about whether the company was in or near bankruptcy (this was a distressed debt fund, after all). For my backup ideas I would make sure to pick companies in different industries in case my interviewer didn't know my company's business well.

You may be tested on current events. If China is hot, a global macro fund may want to see that you know what's going on in that country and what your views are on the currency. To see that you are on top of the latest news, you may be asked what appeared on the front page of that day's *Wall Street Journal.* Answering that correctly may guarantee that you move on in the process, whereas stumbling on the answer could be damaging to your chances.

One candidate described two kinds of case studies in interviews—those that are given on the spot and others that are to be taken home. For on-the-spot case studies, a candidate will usually be given financial statements, annual and quarterly statements, a press release or two about the company, and some data such as where the stock or bonds are trading. At that point you are given two hours to come back with an idea. The purpose is not to return with a buy recommendation. That would be impossible in such a short period of time. The idea is to see what you would do given all this information, how you would come up with the key points that will help your decision-making process, and how you would then pursue those points. They don't want someone who spends eight hours on the exercise and comes up with some minute bit of information that doesn't interest anyone.

For many, the take-home case studies are more challenging. If you are given two weeks to come back with a presentation you may be tempted to work on it 24/7 and present a long and detailed thesis. One MBA candidate we know pointed out that it can be tough to dedicate two weeks in the fall of your last year, which is the height of recruiting season, to do a case study for one interview. The nature of the on-the-spot case studies can make them more stressful, but at least you know what they expect of you, he said.

Chapter XIII

COMPENSATION

You've probably heard of the huge compensation packages of some star hedge fund professionals. But let's be realistic: The really big earners are the head portfolio managers and founders of the funds. To be sure, your compensation could be strong compared to other areas of financial services. As a junior-level analyst or trader, however, you should not expect to hit it big in your first few years on the job.

Compensation for most junior hedge fund professionals is comprised of annual base salaries and cash bonuses. Base salaries at most hedge funds do not fluctuate much from year to year. In fact, from our experience they remain in a relatively tight band, with only minimal increases from one year to the next. Thus, the majority of an individual's compensation comes from his/her bonus. The people you see earning millions do so because they get a percentage of the fund's profits.

When thinking about compensation, it's important that you understand where hedge funds get the money they use to pay their professionals. As we pointed out in Chapter I, most funds charge a 1% to 2% management fee. It's this fee that is used to pay the salaries of most of the hedge fund professionals. The large bonuses that you've read about typically come out of the incentive fee (percentage of the fund's profits). This fee can be anywhere from 15% to 50%, but generally ranges from 15% to 30% with the norm being 20%. Take the case of a $1 billion fund with a 2% management fee and a 25% incentive fee. This fund will have $20 million with which to pay overhead. If the fund posts a 10% profit ($100 million), its incentive fee will total $25 million.

There is no guarantee that a hedge fund will post consistent returns year in and year out. It's possible that a fund can be up one year (and pay significant bonuses), but down the next (and pay smaller bonuses). As we also explained earlier, funds that have a high-water mark provision may not even collect an incentive fee if they are performing poorly. Remember, high-water marks mandate that a hedge fund must recover any losses before it can charge incentive fees, so if a fund loses $100 million one year but earns $150 million the next, any performance fee for the second year will be based on only the $50 million gain that exceeded the prior year's loss.

From our experience, the primary driver of base salaries at hedge funds is fund size. Not surprisingly, base salaries tend to increase as assets under management increase, which is a reflection of higher management fees and a nonproportionate increase in staff size. Base salaries are not significantly affected by a firm's investment performance, but bonuses are. Bonuses tend to be greater at larger funds (the bigger P&L creates more opportunities for bigger bonuses) and, as one would expect, at top-performing funds as well.

HEDGE FUNDS VERSUS PRIVATE EQUITY

Since hedge funds and private equity funds are now competing for some of the same talent, it is good to know the compensation structure of each. Hedge funds are more affected by short-term fluctuations in the stock market than are private equity funds. In contrast to private equity, which is more of a long-term equity game, hedge funds are marked to market daily; bonuses are calculated based on annual profits. In private equity, the big payoff comes further down the line in the form of carry when a fund is successful and is bringing in profits from its investments.

INVESTMENT PROFESSIONALS

Compensation for investment professionals, or analysts, has been rising over the past few years, with much of the increase due to the demand for top talent and the relative lack of qualified professionals to fill those positions. Recently, we've observed that the competition to find top candidates is not just among competing hedge funds. Private equity funds are also competing for some of the same talent, and the investment banks themselves are looking to retain analysts as their own activities have picked up.

The competition for talent has been especially evident for analysts coming out of investment banking, and to a lesser extent from consulting programs. We've seen elite analysts from leading investment banking programs with one to three years of experience receiving offers with base salaries of $90,000 to $110,000 and in extreme cases up to $150,000 from the large funds. Bonuses for those same incoming analysts can total 100% to 200% of their base salaries.

As we pointed out earlier, hedge funds are not hesitant to make offers and entice analysts to pull out of their banking programs early. While the offers they receive may not match what those analysts would get if they stayed in their programs and landed a position with a hedge fund after the end of their two-year commitment, the offers are still more than they earn at the banks during the program. And they get into a hedge fund that much sooner.

The overriding feeling in hedge funds has become: If the fund does well, its employees will do well also, and the investment professionals can be some of the major beneficiaries. Here are some of the trends we've noticed:

Table 13.1 Compensation Breakdown by Experience

	1-4 YEARS OF EXPERIENCE	5-9 YEARS OF EXPERIENCE	10+ YEARS OF EXPERIENCE
Investment Professionals			
Average Base Salary	$126,000	$187,000	$221,000
Average Bonus	$166,000	$490,000	$765,000
Total Cash Compensation	$292,000	$677,000	$986,000
Traders			
Average Base Salary	$114,000	$148,000	$174,000
Average Bonus	$115,000	$185,000	$320,000
Total Cash Compensation	$229,000	$333,000	$494,000

Source: The 2008 Hedge Fund Compensation Report (published by Glocap Search, Institutional Investor News and Lipper Tass).

Note: These are averages for all funds regardless of size, performance, or investment style. The data does not include compensation from any form of ownership.

- As a general rule of thumb, the more assets under management and the better the performance, the more money investment professionals will make.
- For 2007/2008, investment professionals with one to four years of experience generally earn base salaries of $75,000 to $135,000. Bonuses typically begin at 100% of base salaries.
- At the five- to nine-year experience level, the 2007/2008 base salary range for investment professionals expands to $125,000 to $200,000, but the real expansion is in bonuses, which can range from $200,000 to $1 million plus, depending on fund performance and the individual's percentage of profit sharing.
- Finally, 2007/2008 base salaries for investment professionals with 10+ years of experience can range from $150,000 to $225,000, but bonuses can be anywhere from $300,000 to several million dollars, depending on the individual's profit share.

Compensation ranges for hedge fund professionals can vary substantially and are driven by asset class and fund size, and in turn by the management fees earned. Table 13.1 gives a more detailed breakdown of average base salaries and cash bonuses for investment professionals (analysts) and traders at hedge funds.

PROFIT-SHARING BONUSES

Nearly all entry-level investment professionals are pure base salary and bonus employees. It's the more seasoned professionals who are paid a percentage of the profits earned on the money they manage (known as their "P&L" or "carve-out"). This is what all junior professionals should aspire to, as it is this second group that takes home significant compensation packages. From our vantage point, the percentage of profits that is paid to investment professionals has been increasing over the past few years as the demand for qualified employees has increased. A typical deal for portfolio managers managing their own book within a hedge fund could pay them 25% to 50% of the firm's incentive fee on their carve-out. As we explained earlier, the incentive fee is typically 20%, but in some cases can be as high as 60% for certain exceptionally high-performing firms.

Glocap Insight The more trading-oriented and larger funds are the ones that are more likely to pay people on their own P&L.

For example, if an individual's book (the amount they manage, or carve out) is $100 million and they earn a 20% return on that carve-out, the firm itself would earn an incentive fee of $4 million (assuming a 20% incentive fee). Therefore, an employee who had a deal giving him/her 50% of his/her P&L would receive $2 million in additional compensation. The point at which an investment professional falls within that 25% to 50% range depends on several factors, including performance, seniority, and type of firm.

TRADERS

As with analysts, total compensation for traders increases as their years of experience rise. From our experience, compensation for traders varies widely, with a definite demarcation between execution traders—those who may simply take orders—and traders who add more value through their own market knowledge and/or their industry contacts.

- In general, execution traders earn base salaries of $70,000 to $200,000, with bonuses that can reach 100% of salaries. As expected, bonuses are highly correlated to performance and rise with better fund performance.
- The more junior execution traders (those with one to four years of experience) can expect base salaries of $55,000 to $120,000. Salaries for those working at the bigger and/or higher-performing hedge funds will be at the higher end of the range. Bonuses are typically 50% to 100% of base salaries at this level.
- For those traders who have a large degree of discretion, compensation can be more in line with that of analysts of the same experience level than with execution-only traders. Thus, the more value-added traders can make significantly more than execution traders.

RISK MANAGEMENT

The increased emphasis on risk management has led to higher compensation for those professionals. As with the more traditional investment professionals, compensation for risk managers, analysts, and programmers is directly affected by their experience, fund performance, and fund size. We have also noticed that hedge funds have found it necessary to pay a premium to attract risk professionals from investment banks. That means:

- Risk analysts can earn packages in the $120,000 to $300,000 range.
- Risk programmers, the most junior professionals in most risk groups, can take home $85,000 to $125,000 in total compensation.

Most risk professionals who make the switch from investment banks or buy-side firms are moving from being one of many people in a large group to one of just a few in a small group. Therefore, despite the added attraction of joining a hedge fund, they have to be compensated for the additional responsibilities.

We know of one candidate who moved to a hedge fund from the buy-side arm of a major Wall Street firm. He went from earning a base salary of $73,000 with a $30,000 bonus to a risk analyst/risk manager position at a hedge fund that paid him $85,000 in salary, a $5,000 signing bonus, and a $40,000 annual bonus.

MARKETERS

Experience is perhaps the single most important factor determining compensation for fund marketers. As experience increases, the role of the marketers changes and the compensation goes up. Fund performance and staff size also affect compensation, but do so at greater degrees as marketing professionals get more senior. Bonuses for the most experienced marketing professionals (fund-raisers) are usually tied to the amount of assets they bring in.

As we explained in Chapter VI, fund marketers typically start out in a client services role then move on to handle investor relations (IR). After several years of total experience they could graduate to a fund-raising role. Fund performance and fund size do not have a considerable impact on compensation for client services and IR/marketing associates. According to our data:

- Total 2007/2008 compensation for client services associates ranges from $80,000 to $120,000, with base salaries of $60,000 to $80,000.
- Total 2007/2008 compensation for IR/marketing associates fluctuates between $130,000 and $300,000, with base salaries accounting for $85,000 to $150,000 of the total.

- For 2007/2008, experienced fund-raisers earn total packages in the $300,000 to $1 million plus range, with base salaries of $150,000 to $250,000 (we've seen outliers earning base salaries of close to $350,000).

ACCOUNTING

Compensation for hedge fund accountants is largely a function of their experience and the performance of the hedge fund. Interestingly, in most cases we have not seen compensation affected dramatically by fund size. In fact, contrary to conventional wisdom, smaller funds often pay more than larger funds to attract quality candidates. The smaller funds feel a need to be more generous because it has been a harder sell for them to get qualified candidates to consider their funds over much larger ones.

The overriding factor that has pushed salaries for accountants higher is the scarcity of qualified candidates. By that we mean it's difficult to find an accountant who wants to remain an accountant. Many junior accountants have been pursuing (and getting) nonaccounting roles at hedge funds. Thus, those accountants who choose to remain in the industry may be targeted by several hedge funds looking to beef up their internal accounting capabilities.

Hedge funds typically base their starting salaries on what accountants earn at the Big Four accounting firms. For the calendar year 2007, junior-level public accountants (those with one to three years of experience) were earning anywhere from $65,000 to $85,000. From our experience, hedge funds will pay 15% to 20% more on average to hire junior accountants from Big Four firms. Of the more junior accounting roles, fund accountants and senior fund accountants typically earn base salaries of $60,000 to $80,000 and $60,000 to $90,000, respectively, with cash bonuses that can range between 20% and 30% of base salaries. Base salaries for accounting managers and assistant controllers can range from $90,000 to $110,000 and from $110,000 to $125,000, with bonuses equal to 20% to 30% of the base salaries.

OPERATIONS

Although compensation ranges can vary for the different operations roles, the main factor that affects overall compensation is a candidate's level of experience. Fund performance and fund size have relatively little impact on compensation, as pay for operations professionals is relatively uniform across most funds. Operations managers and operations specialists can expect to earn base salaries of $80,000 to $110,000 and $60,000 to $80,000, respectively, with bonuses of 25% to 30% of those totals.

Chapter XIV

WORKING WITH A RECRUITER

Some candidates carry out a successful job search on their own; however, most find the best strategy is to combine their own efforts with a recruiter that specializes in hedge funds. In this chapter we give an overview on how to best work with a recruiter.

As we've said earlier, recruiters play a large role in hedge fund job searches and we wouldn't be successful if we didn't reach out to candidates. It's the way we work and how we continually source top candidates for our clients. If you're a top-ranked first-year analyst at an investment bank (or in rare cases at a consulting firm) you can expect to get calls from a recruiter. Although recruiters traditionally don't work with business school students, we are available for counseling and do work with those people who have been in the workforce for a few years. If you're at the top of your analyst class, don't be surprised if you get calls from multiple recruiters. Either way, you will have to decide if the recruiters are calling with the jobs you want. For those of you whose phones don't ring, it doesn't mean that you are not desirable. You may just have to reach out to recruiters yourself.

Given the nature of what we do, we are on the receiving end of a lot of resumes, and candidates often want to know what we look for when we sift through those resumes and decide who to bring in for a meeting. A quick glance at a resume will tell us right away if someone has the right resume variables for a particular position. What we can't tell is if you have the right nonresume variables (e.g., personality, demeanor, articulateness, etc.). So, we will typically agree to meet those candidates whose resumes reflect the variables our clients want so we can then determine if you have the correct nonresume attributes. Thus, the best way to get in the door with us is to make sure your resume shows the relevant industry experience (investment banking, buy side, etc.) and a strong academic background, both undergraduate and graduate (if applicable).

If you lack the relevant background, then securing an interview with a recruiter will be tough. In this situation we'd strongly suggest using your personal network (get recommended to the recruiter by somebody we know and respect) or persistence (to a point). In our case, the recommendation would carry a lot more weight if it comes from the person directly. For example, rather than writing and saying, "Joe Smith said I should give you a call." It would be much better if Joe called and said, "I know someone who I think you should meet. His background may not be perfect, but he's a great guy and has what it takes." If we respect Joe we would call you in for a meeting. Even if a recruiter won't agree to meet you in person, if you get through to them on the phone they will likely at least give you some advice and speak with you for a few minutes. Try that when all else fails.

In an industry such as hedge funds there historically has not been a shortage of high-quality people looking to break in, and therefore recruiters are often hired by the client not only to find candidates but to screen those candidates for the optimal fit and caliber.

TIPS FOR GETTING THE MOST OUT OF A RECRUITER

Working with a recruiter can be a challenge. Here are few tips we have found to be particularly helpful.

Make the Introduction

Introduce yourself briefly—this can be by e-mail or phone (for Glocap you would register on our web site). As we said, if you can get a high-end recommendation you will likely fare better. In a recruiter interview, you should start with a description of your background and highlight your major strengths. Explain why you are looking to leave your current position and note your potential job interests. Do not restate your resume. If applicable, mention how you got the recruiter's name (referred by a colleague, etc.); this should better help you get under the recruiter's radar. Better yet, if that colleague got placed by the recruiter or had a close relationship, have them call the recruiter to make the introduction. If this is a blind introduction, ask for a referral to a more appropriate recruiter at the firm in case the person does not cover your area of interest.

We'll Call If We See a Match

Professional recruiters will usually respond to a direct inquiry from you as a courtesy. You'll likely receive a call as well if your background is a good match for a particular client with whom we are *currently* working. If the recruiter doesn't have any positions to discuss with you, they might still want to speak with you to learn more about your background for future reference or will simply hold on to your information until a search opens that does match your background.

No Practice Interviews

If you're presented an opportunity, be honest about your level of interest. If it's your dream job or your qualifications match the job perfectly, explain why to the recruiter—it could help them better market your background. If you haven't heard of the firm or you need to contemplate the opportunity further, you should feel free to take a few days to research and think it over. Do not take an interview for practice or informational purposes. Recruiters are sensitive to wasting their client's time. If you decide to pass on an interview, briefly explain why and perhaps have a follow-up conversation to hone in further on your job search interests.

Recruiters as Resources

Think of recruiters as a valuable resource. They may have additional insight into a particular firm and position, which could help you evaluate the opportunity and prepare for an interview. A good recruiter who spends enough time getting to know you as well as the client firm is in a great position to find the all-important fit. Recruiters are usually entrenched in the market and as such can be good sources of information about how a hedge fund is perceived in the market.

Give Feedback

If you go on a client interview, let the recruiter know how the meeting went and if you're still interested or would like to bow out of the process. Be specific about how the opportunity does or does not meet your interests. It's fair to ask if the recruiter has received feedback as well. Most recruiters will share constructive feedback they have received from the client, but please, don't shoot the messenger!

Keep Us in the Loop

Stay in touch with your recruiter if your search criteria have changed at all, if you're approaching final rounds at another firm, if you were recently promoted, or if there were other general changes to your profile. When checking in with a recruiter, be specific. If you'd like to inquire about the status of a certain job, note the firm's name or job/reference number. Try to avoid just touching base in general—this usually adds little to no value to the recruiter or your job search.

Know What You Want

Most successful candidates are specifically focused on what they want. It's okay to have job interests in several different areas provided that your skill set really does leverage that far, but try to tier your interests and identify which opportunities are most interesting and fitting for you.

Don't Play Hard to Get

Be responsive. If you are contacted by a recruiter, make a point to follow up as quickly as possible. If you're slow to respond, the recruiter may think you are uninterested, out of the market, or even difficult to represent. Remember, you need to first make a good impression on the recruiter in order to be introduced to the recruiter's client.

Hiring Firms Have the Final Word

Our clients (the hiring firms) are the ones who pay recruiting fees. As such they can define as narrowly as they please the set of resumes and backgrounds that they are interested in seeing from a recruiter. As recruiters there is little point for us to stray far from the specifications that our clients provide. In that scenario, more often than not the question is not whether you can learn the job, but rather if you have the background the client wants. While you may be a 75% fit for the job, someone else could be a 98% fit and you just may not stack up competitively enough.

No Attitude, Please

Remember that you are one of many candidates with whom the recruiter is working. You can certainly feel confident about being a strong candidate, but having an attitude that conveys "You will make money off of me" is not a good way to get the attention you want. A wise recruiter knows that a great candidate can also be a potential future client. When working with a recruiter your job search is a collaborative effort!

Appendix A

RESOURCES

NEWS PUBLICATIONS/TRADE JOURNALS

There are numerous publications and Web sites that cover the hedge fund industry. In addition to keeping you up-to-date on news and events, some have their own job postings.

Alternative Investment News
www.iialternatives.com
Subscription-based weekly newsletter

The Deal/The Daily Deal
www.thedeal.com
Subscription-based newsletter

Financial News Online
www.efinancialnews.com
Subscription-based online news

Hedge Fund Alert
www.hfalert.com
Subscription-based weekly newsletter

Hedge Fund Daily
www.dailyii.com
A free daily aggregate of industry news put out by Institutional Investor

HedgeFund.net
www.hedgefund.net
Free source for hedge fund information, with detailed fund data, news, and editorial content

Hedge Fund Trades
www.djnewsletters.com
Subscription-based weekly newsletter

HedgeWeek
www.hedgeweek.com
Subscription-based news

Lipper HedgeWorld
www.hedgeworld.com/community/build_website.cgi
Community for investors, managers, and service providers

TRADE JOURNALS

Absolute Return Magazine
www.hedgefundintelligence.com
Monthly magazine published by HedgeFund Intelligence

Alpha Magazine
www.iimagazine.com
Monthly magazine published by Institutional Investor

HedgeFund Intelligence
www.hedgefundintelligence.com
Provides industry data and publishes Absolute Return, AsiaHedge, EuroHedge, InvestHedge, *and* AfricaHedge *magazines*

Journal of Alternative Investments
www.iijai.com
Academic quarterly journal published by Institutional Investor

SUGGESTED BOOKS

Bernstein, Peter L. *Against the Gods: The Remarkable Story of Risk.* New York: John Wiley & Sons, Inc., 1996; new pap. ed. 1998.

Buffett, Warren. *The Essays of Warren Buffett: Lessons of Corporate America. Carolina Academic Press, 2001.*

Burrough, Bryan, and John Heylar, *Barbarians at the Gate.* HarperCollins, 1990, 2003.

Graham, Benjamin. *The Intelligent Investor: A Book of Practical Counsel.* Harper & Row, New York, 1973.

Graham, Benjamin, and David Dodd. *Security Analysis.* New York: McGraw-Hill, 1934.

Greenblatt, Joel. *The Little Book That Beats the Market.* Hoboken, NJ: John Wiley & Sons, Inc., 2006.

Greenblatt, Joel. *You Can Be a Stock Market Genius*. New York: Fireside Books, 1997.

Hull, John C. *Options, Futures and Other Derivatives*. New York: Prentice Hall, 2000.

Kiev, Ari. *Trading to Win*. New York: John Wiley & Sons, Inc., 1998.

Klarman, Seth. *Margin of Safety: Risk Averse Value Investing Strategies for the Thoughtful Investor*. 2000, Paperback Beard Books.

Lewis, Michael. *Liar's Poker*. New York: Penguin Books, 1989.

Lowe, Janet. *Damn Right! Behind the Scenes with Berkshire Hathaway Billionaire Charlie Munger*. New York: John Wiley & Sons, Inc., 2000.

Lowenstein, Roger. *When Genius Failed: The Rise and Fall of Long Term Capital Management*. New York: Random House Trade Paperbacks, 2000.

Lynch, Peter. *Beating the Street*, New York: Fireside, 1994.

Lynch, Peter and Rothschild, John. *Learn to Earn*. New York: John Wiley & Sons, Inc., 1996.

Malkiel, Burton G. *A Random Walk Down Wall Street*. New York: W.W. Norton & Company, 2003.

Nicholas, Joseph. *Investing in Hedge Funds: Strategies for the New Marketplace*. New York: Bloomberg Press, 2005.

Siegel, Jeremy J. *Stocks for the Long Run*. New York: McGraw-Hill, 2002.

Soros, George. *The Alchemy of Finance*. Hoboken, N.J: John Wiley & Sons, Inc., 1987.

Swensen, David F. *Pioneering Portfolio Management: An Unconventional Approach to Institutional Investment*. New York: The Free Press, 2000.

Taleb, Nassim Nicholas. *Fooled by Randomness: The Hidden Role of Chance in Life and in the Markets*. New York: Texere, 2004.

Tuckman, Bruce. *Fixed Income Securities*, New York: John Wiley & Sons, Inc., 2002.

OTHER RESOURCES

Hedge Fund Research Inc.
www.hfr.com
Aggregates, disseminates, and analyzes alternative investment information. Also produces a database of hedge fund performance, an industry report, and various market indices.

Hedge Fund News
www.hedgefundnews.com
Provides news and databases

HedgeCo.net
www.hedgeco.net/hedge-fund-index-AtoC.htm
Free online information portal

Hedge Fund Center
www.hedgefundcenter.com/index.cfm
Provides news and data on the industry

HedgeFund.net
www.hedgefund.net
Hedge fund news and performance data

HedgeFundRegulation.com
www.hedgefundregulation.com
Information source for regulation and compliance with links to news sources

HEDGE FUND ASSOCIATIONS

Alternative Investment Research Centre (AIRC)
www.cass.city.ac.uk/airc/index.html

Asian Hedge Fund Association
www.asiahfa.com/

Hedge Fund Association
www.thehfa.org/

Hedge Fund Marketing Alliance
www.hedgefundmarketing.org/

Managed Funds Association
www.mfainfo.org/

DIRECTORIES/DATABASES

Eurekahedge
www.eurekahedge.com
Also publishes:

- Asia and Japan Hedge Fund Directory
- European Hedge Fund Directory
- Global Fund of Funds Directory
- North American Hedge Fund Directory

Private Equity Info
www.privateequityinfo.com/hedgefund.php
A searchable database of U.S. registered hedge funds

INDEXES AND RESEARCH

There are several indexes that measure hedge fund performance. These are some of the most often listed indexes.

Credit Suisse/Tremont Fund Indexes
www.hedgeindex.com

Greenwich Alternative Investments
www.greenwichai.com
Provides hedge fund–related investment products and services, including research, indexing, investment management, and advisory services

Hedge Fund Consistency Index
www.hedgefund-index.com
Profiles and ranks hedge funds, available to qualified investors

Hedge Fund Research
www.hedgefundresearch.com

The Hennessee Group
www.hennesseegroup.com

MSCI Hedge Fund Indices
www.mscibarra.com/products/indices/hf/press.jsp

Appendix B

SAMPLE RESUMES

Resume A

Profile

Pre-MBA: Bulge-Bracket Banker Lands at a Distressed Debt Fund

(see CASE STUDY 1)

Recruiter's Perspective
- Top name school
- Solid SATs/GPA
- M&A experience
- Worked on large deals

Pluses
Interested in investing

EXPERIENCE

BULGE-BRACKET INVESTMENT BANK
Financial Analyst, Mergers & Acquisitions, Investment Banking Division

New York, NY
July 2005 – February 2006

- Performed detailed financial analyses on potential acquisitions, leveraged buyouts, and divestitures
- Constructed valuation models, including discounted cash flow, comparable company, and precedent transaction analysis
- Assessed the effects of multiple operational scenarios and capital structure alternatives on potential mergers
- Created client presentations illustrating strategic alternatives
- Worked closely with management to prepare offering materials, including management presentations
- Evaluated companies' defense profiles for vulnerabilities for both hostile buy-side and hostile defense transactions
- Became familiar with multiple industries and subsectors

SELECTED WORK EXPERIENCE

- Advised a company on the acquisition of a supplier
  - Created a dynamic, bottom-up financial model for valuation based on public information and key metrics, incorporating sum-of-the-parts discounted cash flow, leveraged buyout, and pro forma merger analyses
  - Performed potential interloper analysis, analyzing the accretion/dilution and value impact on numerous possible bidders
  - Organized materials to prepare an indicative bid
- Advised company on the sale of approximately $1.5 billion in assets
  - Created a full pro forma model capable of multiple operating scenarios, as well as LBO and DCF analyses
  - Performed due diligence on assets, and incorporated research and analysis into modeling effort
- Advised company on the divestiture of approximately $3 billion in assets
  - Created a model to value the assets using both base-case metrics and bidders' implied assumptions, particularly those revolving around the valuation of a major outstanding pension liability
  - Managed the flow of information between the company and interested parties
- Advised company on hostile defense planning
  - Analyzed pro forma accretion/dilution impact to potential bidders based on internal company financials and public information
  - Prepared management presentation describing detailed financial and qualitative analysis of potential bidders and potential synergies as seen by bidding parties
  - Worked with the client to establish measures to defend against a hostile bid

MAJOR AUTOMOTIVE COMPANY
Summer Financial Analyst

Summer 2004

- Built financial model to more accurately account for ocean freight shipments from overseas suppliers to Fortune 5 company
- Worked closely with suppliers and company's in-house technology department to create a new system to facilitate Sarbanes-Oxley compliance

EDUCATION

IVY LEAGUE UNIVERSITY

August 2001–May 2005

B.S. with Honors; GPA: 3.91/4.00
Dean's List Spring 2002 through Fall 2004
SAT: Math – 800, Verbal – 780; National Merit Finalist

OTHER

- Certified General Securities Registered Representative (Series 7) and Uniform Securities Agent (Series 63)
- High level of skill with Microsoft Excel; background in C++, Stata, and Business Objects
- Course work in Finance, Investments, Econometrics, Intermediate Accounting, Computer Science, Linear Algebra, Multivariable Calculus, and Group Theory
- Ivy League recruiting team. Assisted with on-campus events, selection, and calls to candidates
- *Language:* Proficient in Spanish
- *Activities & Interests:* Hockey, investing, chess, economics, mathematics, and writing

Pre-MBA: Getting In from a Second-Tier Bank

(see CASE STUDY 2)

Recruiter's Perspective
- Top name school
- Solid SATs/GPA
- Leveraged finance experience
- Worked at a hedge fund
- Well rounded (varsity athlete)
- VP fraternity

PROFESSIONAL EXPERIENCE
MID-TIER INVESTMENT BANK, New York, NY
Investment Banking Analyst – Leveraged Finance Group   *June 2005 – Nov. 2006*
- Analyzed transactions by providing capital structure/valuation advice and assessing viability of business plans/forecasts, barriers to entry, and market competitiveness
- Presented and defended proposed transactions in capital commitment committees
- Participated in deal teams to advise clients on leveraged buyouts, recapitalizations, strategic alternatives, and equity and debt capital raising
- Constructed financial models, including leveraged buyouts, recapitalizations, mergers and acquisitions, and discounted cash flow
- Examined company, industry, and market dynamics to evaluate potential acquisitions and divestitures for clients
- Transaction experience:
  - ➤ Sole Book Running Manager on $170 million of Senior Notes and $25 million of Senior Subordinated Discount Notes
  - ➤ Represented three private equity firms in bid for major media company

SMALL HEDGE FUND, Greenwich, CT   *May 2004 – August 2004*
Summer Analyst
- Evaluated potential investment opportunities in the small-cap high-yield bond market
- Performed company and industry research
- Assisted in managing relationships with investors
- Analyzed the effectiveness of the firm's hedging positions by running scenarios based on historical market events, such as 9/11 and the Russian debt default
- Examined the usefulness of different hedging strategies

EDUCATION
IVY LEAGUE UNIVERSITY   *2005*
Bachelor of Arts: Major – Political Science
- Cumulative GPA 3.6/4.0
- Relevant Coursework Included: Accounting, Micro- and Macroeconomics, International Trade Theory and Policy, Politics and Markets, and Multivariable Calculus
- Men's Varsity Swimming (2001–2004)
- Vice President, Fraternity (2005)

PRIVATE BOARDING SCHOOL   *2001*
- SAT: 1,480 (770 Math, 710 Verbal)
- Graduated with distinction in Math, Chemistry, and Physics
- Tri-varsity athlete

Resume C

Profile
Pre-MBA: Making It with a Liberal Arts Degree
(see CASE STUDY 3)

EXPERIENCE

July 2005 to July 2007

BOUTIQUE INVESTMENT BANK   New York, NY
Investment Banking Analyst
- Performed financial and operational modeling to evaluate the accretion/dilution, cash flow, and leverage effects of mergers, acquisitions, leveraged buyouts, and corporate restructurings
- Participated in client meetings, due diligence, and internal committee meetings
- Managed the due diligence and site visits associated with sell-side transactions
- Drafted management presentations and company profiles

Selected transaction experience:
- Advised a major corporation on its proposed reorganization (six mergers) and eventual Initial Public Offering
  - Built a valuation model in order to properly value the stand-alone regions singularly and on a pro forma basis in order to merge six of the regions into one entity and pursue a global float
  - Worked with company Board of Directors, company executives, and management in order to accurately gauge the impact of legal liability and drafted materials proposing an adequate financial structure to maximize value and mitigate forthcoming legal liabilities
- Advised manufacturing company on its $1 billion+ acquisition of rival
  - Conducted stand-alone valuation, accretion/dilution, and noncore asset valuation for the purchase
  - Maintained a purchase price spread analysis during the ongoing regulatory approval period
- Advised a financial buyer on the acquisition of natural gas pipeline assets (approx. $250mm)
  - Constructed an operating model, discounted cash flow analysis, and LBO to project revenues associated with the processing of natural gas and sale of natural gas products
  - Participated in due diligence and site visits on behalf of the client
- Advised company on its sale to another company
  - Constructed a working capital model to project final adjustments made to the purchase price
  - Drafted and organized materials for the Management Presentation along with coordinating the data room

May 2004 to August 2004

LEADING INVESTMENT BANK   New York, NY
Investment Banking Summer Analyst
- Valued companies and their comparables using discounted cash flows
- Gauged demand for potential equity transactions and helped price equity deals
- Tracked market conditions and gauged the proper size for potential equity transactions
- Built and maintained a database of venture capital sponsored Initial Public Offerings since 1999

Selected transaction experience:
- Pitch for Bank IPO
- Entertainment Company Follow-on Offering ($200mm)

May 2003 to August 2003

NOT-FOR-PROFIT   Washington, DC
Visiting Fellow
- Compiled research on the interaction between informal markets and financial institutions
- Wrote and published an internal working paper

EDUCATION

IVY LEAGUE UNIVERSITY
Bachelor of Arts, May 2005. Double Major in History and Latin American Studies
Cumulative GPA: 3.70 / Major GPA: 3.90, 3.95 respectively
- Graduated with Distinction in both majors
- Wrote Senior Thesis for each major
- Member of varsity crew
- Founded fraternity

HIGH SCHOOL
- Graduated in top 3% of class
- 700/700 SATs
- State Champion/Record Holder in Track and Cross Country

OTHER

Interests: Fishing, golf, history, traveling
Languages: Spanish, Portuguese (Spanish a native language)

Profile
Pre-MBA:
A Typical Banking Hire
(see CASE STUDY 4)

Recruiter's Perspective
- Top name school
- Good SATs/GPA
- M&A experience
- Solid deal experience

PROFESSIONAL EXPERIENCE

BULGE-BRACKET INVESTMENT BANK
Financial Analyst, Global Mergers and Acquisitions
Senior Financial Analyst, Global Industrial Investment Banking

NEW YORK, NY
July 2000 – July 2002
July 2002 – June 2003

- Performed comparable companies, precedent transactions, DCF, and LBO analyses. Examined financial outlook of companies on stand-alone and pro forma combined/recapitalized bases. Built detailed models to assist to clients to evaluate business plans.
- Prepared offering memoranda and marketing materials for capital markets and sell-side advisory engagements. Created presentations to evaluate strategic alternatives and explore new business development opportunities.

Selected projects and transactions:

- $1.1 billion sale of pharmaceutical comapany
- Acquisition of selected manufacturing and sales distribution assets of major automotive company
- Sale of industrial company
- $2.1 billion sale of pharmaceutical company
- Divestiture efforts of plastic packaging division by major consumer packaging company
- $125 million mandatory convertible notes offering for shipping company
- $250 million senior subordinated notes offering and $550 million senior secured credit facilities arrangement for packaging company

EDUCATION

IVY LEAGUE UNIVERSITY

- Bachelor of Science in Economics with concentration in Finance and Information Systems, May 2000
    - Graduated Magna Cum Laude
    - Cumulative GPA: 3.64/4.00
    Finance GPA: 3.80/4.00
    SAT: 780 (Math), 670 (Verbal)

ADDITIONAL

- Proficient in Korean
- Computer skills in Microsoft Excel, Word, PowerPoint, and several financial and informational databases

Resume E

Profile
Pre-MBA: Swapping the Sell Side for a Long/Short Fund
(see CASE STUDY 7)

EXPERIENCE:
- **BULGE-BRACKET INVESTMENT BANK,** July 2004 – January 2006

   EQUITY-LINKED ORIGINATION, STRUCTURED PRODUCTS
   - Priced and structured convertible bonds, options, option spreads, forwards, and futures.
   - Structured stock buyback and issuances, and other corporate derivatives.
   - Explained products and ideas to investment bankers and clients.
   - Analyzed market trends and case studies.
   - Prepared presentation materials and other documents.

   IN-HOUSE OPTIONS TRADING GROUP
   - Priced and traded listed and OTC options and structured products.
   - Performed statistical analysis.
   - Performed portfolio and single-position risk management.
   - Worked on strategy formation regarding structured products and volatility/asset management.

   TRAINING PROGRAM PARTICIPANT
   - Training and rotational program. Three months of classes and licensing examinations. Included rotations in the ELO, Derivatives Marketing, Convertible Sales, Cash Trading, and Options groups.

   TOP 50 UNIVERSITY, Fall 2002 – Spring 2004

   TEACHING ASSISTANT, Money and Banking
   - Taught undergraduate money and banking recitations (4 sections, 110 students).

   RESEARCH ASSISTANT
   - Conducted research and statistical analysis on defense contractors.

   NON-U.S.-BASED INDUSTRIAL DEVELOPMENT BANK—CORPORATE FINANCE DIVISION, Summer 2001
   - Conducted research and performed valuation analysis on the local automotive and energy industries.

   GLOBAL TELECOM EQUIPMENT COMPANY, Summer 2000
   - Operational Services (OS) Department System Support Staff.

EDUCATION:

Top 50 University, 2002–2004
M.S. Economics (Concentration in Finance and Statistics) **GPA: 3.5**
GMAT: 740 GRE: Analytical: **800** Quantitative: **800**
Courses Included: Managerial Economics, Advanced Macroeconomics, Mathematical Economics, Advanced Macroeconometrics, Econometrics, Advanced Investments, Investments and Portfolio Management, Forecasting.

Small Liberal Arts College, 1998–2002
Double major, Computer Science and Economics
GPA (Econ): 3.8. Spring 2002

Non-U.S. High School
High School Cumulative GPA: 88.03/100 12/149. 1991–May 1998

Computer Skills:
Environment: Unix/Windows/Linux/Mac OS
Programming Languages: Java/HTML/JavaScript/C
SAS, SPSS, Stata, Minitab, Shazam, MS Office, and other applications

Languages:
- English (fluent), Turkish (fluent), German (competent)

167

Profile
Post-MBA: From Private Equity into Hedge Funds
(see CASE STUDY 12)

May 2003–
Feb 2005
	LARGE PE FUND
	Associate, Turnaround and Restructuring Private Equity
	• Investment professional at private equity fund
	• Developed detailed LBO models, distressed debt purchasing models, and cash forecasting models
	• Negotiated legal documents and drafted internal investment committee memoranda
	• Supervised and coordinated efforts of accountants, consultants, lawyers, and investment bankers
	• Completed intensive Troubled Company Restructuring and Financial Modeling Training
	
	Transaction Experience
	  - ***Corporate Orphan*** – Acquired two companies from parent company and implemented an aggressive cost cutting plan
	  - ***Distressed Debt Purchase*** – Acquired $37 million of distressed debt at a 40% discount to market, giving company a blocking position, and helped drive turnaround and restructuring activities
	  - ***Refinancing*** – Completed a $76 million asset-backed refinancing that provided company with enough liquidity to operate on an ongoing basis
	  - ***Bankruptcy Auction*** – Participated in the bankruptcy auction for home health care provider

Jul 2000–
Apr 2003
	BULGE-BRACKET INVESTMENT BANK **NEW YORK, NY**
	Analyst Merchant Banking
	• Investment professional at leading merchant banking franchise
	• Conducted all aspects of private equity investing, including deal sourcing, detailed financial analysis, industry analysis, due diligence, structuring, financing, and portfolio monitoring
	• Developed comprehensive financial models, including acquisition/disposition and leveraged buyout, and conducted various valuation analyses utilizing discounted cash flow, comparable transaction, and sum-of-the-parts methods
	
	Transaction Experience
	  - ***Management Buyout*** – Aided management in the acquisition of company with over $100 million in revenues
	  - ***Follow-On Acquisitions*** – Completed two geographically strategic follow-on acquisitions with $20 million in revenues
	  - ***Merger*** – Merged two companies to form one with over $300 million in revenues
	  - ***Refinancing*** – Refinanced the consolidated debt of four companies

Jan 1999– Aug 1999	**LEADING HOTELS CHAIN** *Analyst, Corporate Acquisitions and Feasibility Group* • Gained M&A experience providing financial analysis for corporate hotel acquisitions and dispositions worldwide
EDUCATION 1996–1999	**IVY LEAGUE UNIVERSITY** • BS, Finance, December 1999 (graduated early)

Profile

Post-MBA:
A Banker Gets In

(see CASE STUDY 15)

PROFESSIONAL HIGHLIGHTS

INVESTMENT BANK (2002–2005)   New York, NY
Mergers & Acquisitions Group

Associate
• Generalist with emphasis on the telecommunications and media sectors
• Advised a consortium of investors on an unsuccessful acquisition of major U.S. corporation
• Advised corporation on its financial and corporate restructuring
• Advised industrial company on repurchasing shares from its largest shareholder

BOUTIQUE INVESTMENT BANK (1999–2000)   New York, NY
Mergers & Acquisitions Group

Analyst
• Identified and analyzed financing opportunities and strategic alternatives for clients in diverse industries
• Executed comparable analyses, DCF, LBO analysis, accretion/dilution, and other financial valuations for various clients
• Advised major client on numerous transactions, including joint-venture negotiations

BULGE-BRACKET INVESTMENT BANK (1996–1998)   New York, NY
Alternative Asset Management Division

Analyst
• Performed merger-arbitrage analysis on deals to which we were exposed through our hedge fund portfolios
• Evaluated internal funds to assess potential exposures and risks to various market conditions
• Identified, evaluated, and interviewed prospective hedge fund managers

Investment Management Division—Capital Markets Research

Equity Analyst
• Participated in portfolio construction and management
• Actively involved in the development of a large-cap growth fund
• Spearheaded the development of a small-cap value fund

ACADEMIC CREDENTIALS

Top Five Business School
Master of Business Administration, May 2002

Top Five University
Degree in Finance, May 1996

PROFESSIONAL EXPERIENCE

HIGH-YIELD ASSET MANAGEMENT FIRM
Vice President, Marketing & Client Service – October 2000 to September 2005

Responsibilities included business development strategy, as well as the identification, qualification, and close of new business opportunities.

Major accomplishments include increasing assets under management from $2.5 billion to $12.3 billion, securing new business with over 50 new clients, and developing relationships with consulting firms.

- Responsible for face-to-face client, reviews and presentation materials, including advising the firm on client objectives, reporting requirements, and restrictions.
- Completion and assembly of Request for Proposals (RFP) questionnaires for prospective accounts.
- Presentation and close of business at finalist presentations for new accounts, including articulation of the unique value of the firm, creation and preparation of marketing materials, as well as final business negotiations.
- Implementation of the strategic portfolio attribution department, facilitating use of FactSet.
- Extensive institutional client contact, proactively addressing special client requests or projects.

BULGE-BRACKET INVESTMENT BANK
Junior Analyst, Assistant Vice President – July 1999 to October 2000
- Compiled results and reports for the high yield client base as well as the high yield research group.
- Constructed and maintained database files in relation to various financial markets.
- Produced weekly and monthly research publications.
- Maintained client contact in relation to firm's index products as well as high yield strategy.

Sales Assistant, High Yield Capital Markets – May 1994 to July 1999
- Assistant to three salespeople servicing institutional clientele in both the syndicate and secondary high yield market, billing and settling high yield trades on a daily basis.
- Sales liaison to clientele in regard to the high yield market, secondary offerings, new issue calendars, new fixed income and equity research, and other fixed income and equity trading desks.
- Worked directly with Legal and Compliance in complying with regulatory issues and NASD rules.

BOUTIQUE INVESTMENT BANK
Sales Assistant, Institutional Equity Sales – May 1993 to May 1994
- Assistant to three salespeople and one director servicing the institutional equity clientele in a newly created department.
- Liaison between offices for various sales and trading functions, providing support to various analysts, traders, and salespeople throughout the Northeast.
- Obtained Series 7 and Series 63 Registrations.

EDUCATION
TOP 150 UNIVERSITY
BBA Business Administration with Management Concentration – May 1993
Recipient of Honors Program Scholarship, Presidential Scholarship

Profile
Risk:
Switching from the Sell Side
(see CASE STUDY 19)

04/2005 – Present   **Bulge-Bracket Bank**
Financial Analytics & Structured Transactions—Vice President   *New York, NY*
• Support agency-backed and whole-loan MBS/CMO trading and research desks.
• Support and enhance pricing models for TBA pools, dollar rolls, and structured products such as CMOs, CDOs, ABSs, and re-REMICs.
• Close collaboration with the quantitative and research groups to derive actual and projected prepayment speeds (PSA, CPP, Life Survivorship), collateral statistics, duration and option-adjusted spreads used for market analysis and trading.
• Provide the pass-through, ARM, and CMO/CDO desks with on-demand analytics and real-time collateral data during trading hours.

08/2001 – 04/2005   **Asset Management Arm of Bank**
Absolute Return Strategies Group—Assistant Vice President
• Calculated performance attribution across various strategies: Equity Long/Short, Convertible Arbitrage, FOF, and Statistical Arbitrage.
• Evaluated and analyzed effects of corporate actions such as dividend adjustments, tender offers, M&A activity, and stock splits on P&L.
• Provided analytics for fund managers, business analysts, and risk managers on current holdings and new and existing investment strategies.
• Provided support, maintenance, and enhancement of real-time trade management and execution systems.

Major Projects:
• **Outdex Fund Optimizer:**
  - Designed an alpha optimizer used by Long/Short Equity fund managers to extract a list of underperforming securities to be omitted from an index tracking fund.
  - Generated a sorted list of securities and their calculated alphas from a chosen index (S&P 500/Russell 1000) by utilizing reported historical returns and volatility figures.
  - Modeled various market conditions by allowing users to specify custom tolerance parameters to yield skewed results for side-by-side comparison.
• **Front Arena Trade Management System adaptation for use with Fund of Hedge Funds trading:**
  - Designed modules to support FOF trading within the existing single-manager trade platform.
  - Accommodated FOF business model of monthly trading by automating several key business procedures, including FIFO accounting for redemptions, real-time performance attribution, liquidity and cash analytics, risk monitoring, and updating market values based on receipt of daily price estimates.

EDUCATION
CFA CANDIDATE – *Current*
Fall 1998 – Spring 2001   **Top 25 University**
BS in Computer Science and Economics

SKILLS AND INTERESTS
• Technical: Perl, SQL, Excel VB/VBA, Bloomberg
• Interests: Stock Picking, Real Estate Speculation, Mock Portfolio Management
• GMAT Score: 730
• Other Languages: Fluent Russian
• Hobbies: Travel, soccer, skiing, fashion

Profile
Risk: Taking a Roundabout Route to Risk
(see CASE STUDY 20)

SUMMARY

- Strategic risk-capital adviser with four years of executive-level risk management experience in hedge fund and investment bank trading environments covering a diverse set of securities and markets.
- Practical skills in building the basic risk management foundation, reporting structure, and risk limits. Detailed insights into using risk management for strategic portfolio decisions, capital allocation, performance measurement, performance improvement, and the structure of the ideal diversified hedge fund firm.
- Strong analytical ability (780 GMAT) and broad financial knowledge (MBA, CFA).

EXPERIENCE

2003–2006　　**BULGE-BRACKET INVESTMENT BANK**　　　　　　　　　　**New York, NY**

Client Portfolio Strategy – Risk Management

- Consulted on risk management for large institutional fixed income trading clients and numerous smaller REIT, and credit arbitrage portfolios.
- Modeled financial data including scenario total returns across large asset/liability portfolios, risk management metrics and VaR, derivative hedging strategies, duration of bank deposits, portable alpha, and CORE+ portfolios.

Firm Proprietary Trading – Risk Management

- Project analysis of trading risk issues and P&L across the entire firm's trading business, working under the Global Head of Market Risk and reporting to the executive committee.
- Redeveloped reporting of main risk metrics (delta, gamma, vega, P&L, VaR, scenarios, etc.) to better highlight emerging risk factors, new trades, and business concerns across firm's equity derivatives business, including market making, arbitrage, and structured and exotic derivatives.
- Designed risk management procedures for growing billion-dollar hedge-fund-linked derivative structures.

2002　　　　　**SMALL HEDGE FUND**　　　　　　　　　　　　　　　**New York, NY**

Analyst – Investment Research

- Performed fundamental analysis and made investment recommendations for event-driven hedge fund investigating opportunities in distressed debt, turnaround, merger, and spin-off situations.
- Financial statement analysis, including FCF modeling, capital structure analysis, reviews of bond covenants, indentures, and footnotes in order to develop a valuation assessment.

1997–2001　　**Technology Industry**

Held front office positions in sales and consulting at Intel, Net Perceptions, and Euro RSCG.

EDUCATION and OTHER

- Top 15 Business School—MBA in Finance (780 GMAT, +99%)
- Small Liberal Arts College, BA in Philosophy
- Certified Financial Analyst
- Member NYSSA, AIMR, IAFE, Mensa, Series 7 and 63 licenses
- Advanced computer skills: Excel, VBA, SQL, Eviews, MatLab, Bloomberg, BondStudio/Yieldbook

Resume K

Profile
Operations:
The Basic Ops Hire
(see CASE STUDY 21)

EDUCATION

Small Canadian University
BA May 2004
Economics/Humanities/Political Science

Non-U.S. University
Management Program, May 2002

WORK EXPERIENCE

Major Wall Street Bank, New York, New York   08/05–03/07
Global Loan Services
• Fund management for hedge funds and alternative investment companies
• Handled all the daily activities (trading, repricings, reconciliations, cash activity, month-end reporting, loan rolling, new borrowings) for six CLO funds with a total of five clients
• Maintained daily contact with clients and agents
• Reconciled cash with trustee and prepared daily cash reports
• Input and maintained all trading activity for large syndicate groups

Second-Tier Sell-Side Firm   01/05–07/05
Trade Accountant, Domestic Equity Trade Assistant
• Worked in Corporate Actions Department
• Processed security entitlements for mergers, spin-offs, stock splits, bankruptcies, and so on, and ensured that they were handled in a timely and efficient manner
• Worked with brokers and traders to help facilitate the transfer of bonds and mutual funds
• Performed audits on funds
• Checked breaks on daily trades and amended any problems
• Software used—Intrader, Sphinx, StreetScape, & Fidessa

Small Architectural Firm   05/04–10/04
Associate Construction Manager
• Helped manage a construction project while also doing the majority of the construction.
• Coordinated time schedules for different contractors.
• Reported job progress to the client.

EXTRACURRICULAR ACTIVITIES AND SKILLS
• Member of Phi Gamma Delta fraternity
• Sport interests: Tennis, sailing, surfing, squash, rowing, mountain biking, swimming, running, fishing, snowboarding
• Other interests: Architecture, cars, traveling, computers, day trading
• Computer skills: Windows, HTML, Photoshop, MS Office, Outlook, Excel, PowerPoint, Bloomberg, Loan IQ, Lotus Notes, CDO Suite

Profile
Accounting:
An Ideal Accounting Hire
(see CASE STUDY 23)

EXPERIENCE

Big Four Accounting Firm, *Assurance Associate*   New York, NY   Sept. 2005–Sept. 2007
- Audited major investment management, private equity, hedge fund, and investment banking firms.
- Used detailed financial analysis and transactional testing procedures to gain assurance on the respective firms' quarterly and year end financial performance.
- Extensive interaction with clients, including chief executives, financial officers, experts, and attorneys during all phases of the audit engagement.
- Working knowledge of investment products such as MBSs, CDOs, swaps, repurchase agreements, equities, and bonds.
- Completed numerous investment management training courses.
- CPA license, summer 2007

Big Four Accounting Firm, *Summer Intern*   Summer 2004
- Audited major technology companies.
- Audited commercial real estate companies.
- Participated in the firm's Intern Development Program.

EDUCATION

West Coast State University   May 2005
Bachelor of Accountancy with Finance/Real Estate
GPA Overall: 3.83

Studied Abroad   Fall 2003
- Studied international business and Spanish; lived with a Spanish family and participated in a European Multinational Business Tour
- Gained working knowledge of Spanish

HONORS
- Magna Cum Laude
- Varsity Football Academic Honor Roll
- School of Business First Honors
- Accounting Departmental First Honors
- Honors Fraternity
- Dean's List Scholarship Recipient
- Fraternity Scholarship Recipient
- Rotary Scholar

ACTIVITIES
Fraternity
- Selected as chapter representative for leadership workshop
- Treasurer
- Kept chapter books and collected fraternal dues
- Created budgets and allocated funds

Varsity Football, 2001–2002: League Academic Honor Role

Interests: Reading, international travel, Spanish, tennis, photography, golf, football